الطريق المضمون إلى **التدارك** و **الإصلاح** للمسلم المسجون

دروس و عبر و فتاوى

THE GUARANTEED PATH TOWARDS

REDEMPTION

AND

RECTIFICATION

FOR THE INCARCERATED MUSLIM

LESSONS, MORALS & VERDICTS

The Guaranteed Path Towards Redemption and Rectification for the
Incarcerated Muslim

ISBN: 978-1-4507-2188-2

First Edition: Rajab 1431/ June 2010

Publisher's Information:
Authentic Statements Publishing
P.O. Box 15536
Philadelphia, Pa 19131
215.382-3382
215.382.3782-Fax

Store:
5312 Market St.
Philadelphia, Pa 19139

Website: www.authenticstatements.com
E-mail: info@authenticstatements.com

Cover Design: Usul Design
E-mail: info@usuldesign.com

Editing and Typesetting: Proof 2 Print
E-mail: proof2print@gmail.com

Please visit our website for upcoming publications, audio/Dvd online catalog, and info on events and seminars, insha Allah.

Table of Contents

Acknowledgement from Authentic Statements

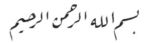

All praises are due to Allaah, we praise Him, we seek His aid and we
seek His forgiveness. We seek refuge with Allaah from the evils of
our souls and from the evil of our actions. Whomsoever Allaah
guides, then there is no one to misguide him and whomsoever
Allaah leaves to go astray then there is no one to guide him. I bear
witness that none has the right to be worshiped except Allaah,
alone, without any partner and that Muhammad is His Slave and
Messenger.

To Proceed:

The Messenger of Allaah, *sallAllaahu 'alaihi wa sallam*, said,

**"Whoever has not thanked the people then he has not thanked
Allaah."** [1]

I would like to sincerely thank our noble brother, Aboo Ramlah
Muhammad Ibn Muneer Abdul Hameed, for all the sacrifices that
were made over the last two years in assisting us in getting our

---

[1] Collected by Aboo Daawood (4811), at-Tirmidhee, Ahmad (5/211/212),
al-Bukhaaree in al-Adabul-Mufrad (33), Ibn Hibbaan (2070), Aboo
Daawood at-Tayaalasee (2491) and al-Albaanee graded it to be authentic in
as-Saheehah (416)

questions answered by the people of knowledge and for his aid in
compiling and translating the information for this book. I invoke
Allaah to increase him in success, guidance, uprightness, firmness
and stability upon the Sunnah. Also, I would like to thank everyone
who assisted with this project. May Allaah, the Exalted, bless us with
success and add this work to our scale of good deeds.

May the peace and blessings of Allaah be upon His final Messenger
Muhammad, his family, his companions and all those who follow
their way until the Last Day.

Aboo Rumaysah Mujaahid Ibn Leroy Smith
Authentic Statements

❀ ❀ ❀

Introduction from Authentic Statements

Al-Hamdulillaahi Rabbil-'Aalameen was Salaatu was Salaamu 'alaa Ashrafil-Anbiyaa' wal-Mursaleen, wa ba'ad.

Salaamun 'alaykum wa rahmatullaahi wa barakaatuhu, Al-Hamdulillaah, this is a very unique book and one of our main points of focus is to stress the importance to our incarcerated brothers on how to use their time wisely in a manner that could benefit them on a daily basis. The realization that some of the illustrious Imaams were incarcerated for periods of their lives are well known and in no way is there any comparison of the two, but the benefits that we received from the writings and books that were done by the illustrious Imaams of the past while incarcerated are of great benefit today.

So, if our brothers would concentrate on issues of *Tauheed,* the correct *'aqeedah,* the sound *minhaj,* the *seerah* of the Prophet, *sallAllaahu 'alaihi wa sallam,* the rules of the *halaal* and *haraam* and all affairs that are important for them from the Islaamic sciences, then by Allaah's permission they could return back to our communities as better Muslims, sons, fathers, etc......

We ask Allaah to extend His mercy to us and you, just as we ask that He preserves all of the living Scholars and that He rewards everyone involved with the publishing of this work in this life and the Hereafter.

Wa Salaamun 'Alaykum wa Rahmatullaahi wa Barakaatuhu,
Your brothers at Authentic Statements

Lecture by Shaykh Hasan Ibn 'Abdul-Wahhaab al-Bannah to the Muslims at Northern State Prison located in Newark, New Jersey on Monday, July 21, 2008

Shaykh Hasan Ibn 'Abdul-Wahhaab Al-Bannah opened by reciting *Khutbatul-Haajah* and then proceeded by quoting the verse from the Qur'aan wherein Allaah says, "*Verily, Allaah forgives not that partners should be set up with Him in worship, but He forgives except that (anything else) to whom He pleases, and whoever sets up partners with Allaah in worship, he has indeed invented a tremendous sin." [Soorah an-Nisaa (4):48].* A Muslim should have a strong and a correct 'aqeedah and to always be with those who have a sound 'aqeedah. Furthermore, he should also learn how to perform the *salaat* (prayer) and *wudoo* (ablution) as the Companions performed them and to stick closely to the people of *tauheed*.

People are of two categories:

1. Those who are ignorant– These are those who act out of ignorance and we should continue to give them *naseehah* (sincere advice) and teach them as well.

2. Those who have knowledge – These are those who act with intelligence.

Everyone is required to give *naseehah* to his Muslim brother in an attempt to call him back to the correct and right way. This is because if we were to leave him, then know that the *Shaytaan* is with those who stray away from the *jamaa'ah* (main body of the Muslims).

It has been narrated that the Messenger of Allaah, May the peace and blessings be upon him, said: **"The best of those who sin are those who make abundant *taubah*."** A Muslim is one who works hard towards righteousness and performs good deeds. Shaykh Hasan continued by telling the brothers that Allaah is the only One Who accepts our prayers and then he made *du'aa* that Allaah bestows His blessings upon the Muslims who were in attendance and also other than them.

So you all should stay away from evil and all evildoers, and if you fall into committing sins then you should always return back by making *taubah*. You should strive to be with good company because bad company will make you fall into more sin. The Messenger of Allaah, May the peace and blessings be upon him, said: **"A Muslim is a mirror for his brother."** The Shaykh continued by explaining to the brothers in attendance that they were being tested, and to not cut off their hope of good, and also not to despair of the mercy of Allaah. Rather, they should call on Allaah to help them during their time of need. He mentioned that there were Muslim scholars from the past who were imprisoned for various reasons such as the likes of Shaykhul Islam Ibn Taymiyyah, Ahmad Ibn Hanbal and Ibnul-Qayyim, May Allaah have mercy upon them. However, these noble scholars did not despair of Allaah's mercy while imprisoned. Therefore, it is imperative for all of you who are incarcerated to be patient and to remain steadfast.

Shaykh Hasan informed those who were in attendance that they were great brothers and that it is ok for them to be upset with their lives at this point due to them being incarcerated and being away from their loved ones, family and their communities. However, the reality of their situation is that Allaah is just and this is the *qadr* (divine decree) that you all have to accept. Therefore, in lieu of your situation, do not be like those on the outside who are free, yet some are engaged in drinking alcohol and running around in a drunken state while others are chasing crazy women and other types of evil sins. All of you in your current state are not affected by these types of things and all praises are due to Allaah. So know that Allaah is keeping you away from all of those types of evil, and *insha Allaah* one day you all will be free.

The Shaykh also reminded everyone in attendance that first and foremost he is reminding himself first of the advice that he is presenting to everyone. He continued by mentioning that Allaah will make a way out for them in their current situation, *insha Allaah*. Therefore, he urged them not to get angry nor give up hope. Rather, they should pray, read the Qur'aan and all types of good righteous deeds, and to always strive to be with those who are on the path of Allaah. If you are successful, then your state may end up similar to that of Imam Ahmad Ibn Hanbal or Ibn Taymiyyah, May Allaah have mercy on them both. The Shaykh also mentioned a statement that Shaykhul Islam Ibn Taymiyyah, May Allaah have mercy on him, once said: "If the one who's incarcerated knew what the people on the outside, who are openly committing sinful acts against Allaah, if they would come to know what they (Ibn Taymiyyah and his students) were doing while in prison, then they would request that they be in prison accompanying them (i.e.... seeking knowledge, praying, fasting and all other types of righteous deeds)."

Shaykh Hasan continued by explaining a very important point by mentioning that to be imprisoned can be looked at as a good thing.

This is due to the fact that there are limitations that place one in a better position to perform righteous deeds and to remain on the straight path. He continued to say that none of the scholars who at some point during their life were imprisoned, they never hated being in prison. In fact they used to enjoy it because they were able to increase themselves in worshiping Allaah. Therefore, it is upon all of the Muslims in attendance to wake up every morning, make *wudoo*, pray and make *du'aa* that Allaah forgives them. Don't let the Shaytaan get the best of you. You must fear Allaah. If you fear Allaah, then he will answer your *du'aa*...

Examples from the Lives of the Salaf[2]

Patience and its Types and Being Pleased with Allaah and His Pre-Ordainment

'Abdullaah Ibn Mas'ood, *radiyAllaahu 'anhu*, said: "It is more beloved to me to bite onto a red coal until it cools than for me to say about something that Allaah has preordained, 'Only if it didn't happen."[3]

Once Ibn 'Abbaas, *radiyAllaahu 'anhumaa*, was on a journey and the news of the death of one of his relatives reached him so he offered two units of voluntary prayer and then said: "We have done what Allaah, the Mighty and Majestic, has ordered us to do: ***"And seek help in patience and prayer"***. *[Soorah al-Baqarah (2):45]*"[4]

---

[2] *Min Akhbaaris-Salaf* (pg. 140-150) with abrigment and adjustment.

TN: The narrations of the Pious Predecessors are to be used as an aid in understanding the texts of the Book and the Sunnah and as a live application of the two. In no circumstance is a narration from one of the Salaf to be used as a legal proof. Instead that which is a legal proof is the consensus of the Salaf. For surely, the Salaf as a whole were exempt from mistake and error and it is totally impossible for them to come to consensus on something incorrect. However, the Salaf as individuals were not exempt from mistake and error. So when reading the likes of these narrations you must keep this in mind.

[3] *Az-Zuhd* of Aboo Daawood (pg. 136)

[4] *As-Shu'ab* (vol. pg. 114)

'Abdul-'Azeez Ibn Abee Rawaad, *rahimahullaah*, lost sight in one of
his eyes for twenty years and neither his wife or children realized it
until one day his son noticed it and cried out to his father: "O
father! You are blind in one eye! He replied to him: "Yes son! Being
pleased with Allaah [and His Pre Ordainment]. He has made your
father blind in one eye since twenty years (ago)!"[5]

It is reported that once Fudayl Ibn 'Iyaad, *rahimahullaah*, said to a
man who was complaining to someone else: "O you! You complain
about the One who shows you mercy to someone that doesn't show
you any mercy."[6]

Sufyaan ath-Thauree, *rahimahullaah*, said: "The one who does not
consider prosperity a misfortune and misfortune adversity is not a
faqeeh."[7]

'Alee Ibn 'Abdil-Hameed, *rahimahullaah*, said: "Those who have the
most patience are those who are patient upon the truth."[8]

Aboo Mas'ood al-Balkhee, *rahimahullaah*, said: "Whoever is afflicted
with a tragedy and he rips up a garment or pounds on his chest then
it is as if he has grabbed a spear and intends to fight his Lord, the
Mighty and Majestic."[9]

---

[5] *Al-Hilyah* (vol. 8/pg. 191)

[6] *As-Siyar* (vol. 6/pg. 439)

[7] *As-Siyar* (vol. 7/pg. 66)

[8] *As-Shu'ab* (pg. 9710)

[9] *Faydul-Qadeer* (vol. 3/pg. 230)

'Umar Ibn 'Abdil-'Azeez, *rahimahullaah*, said: "I don't want nothing from the drunkenness of death to be lightened on me, because it is from the last things that will expiate the sins of the Muslim."[10]

Shurayh al-Qaadee, *rahimahullaah*, said: "Indeed, I am afflicted with a misfortune and I thank Allaah; I thank Allaah that it wasn't a greater calamity, I thank Him for providing me with patience upon it, I thank Him for granting me the success to say: Indeed we belong to Allaah and unto Him we will return, for the reward that I hope from it, and I thank Him for it not being a calamity in my religion."[11]

Sufyaan, *rahimahullaah*, said: "It used to be said, 'The Believer needs patience, just like he needs food and drink."[12]

Sufyaan Ibn 'Uyaynah, *rahimahullaah*, said: "The slaves have never been given anything better than patience; because of it they will enter Paradise."[13]

Narrated 'Uthmaan Ibn 'Attaa, *rahimahullaah*, from his father who said: "Verily, Paradise is enclosed with patience and disliked things, therefore it cannot be approached except from a gate of patience or something disliked. And Hell has been branched off with lusts and

---

[10] *Taslilatu Ahlil-Masaa'ib* (pg. 37)

[11] *As-Siyar* (vol. 4/pg. 105)

[12] *As-Sabr* (pg. 81)

[13] *As-Sabr* (pg. 60)

pleasures; therefore it cannot be approached except by a lust or pleasure."[14]

Wahb Ibn Munabbih, *rahimahullaah*, said: "Whoever is afflicted with some type of calamity then Allaah has put him through the path of the Prophets, May prayers and salutations be upon them."[15]

Mutarrif Ibn 'Abdillaah, *rahimahullaah*, said: "It isn't befitting for someone to climb and throw himself from atop of a steep well and then say, 'This was decreed upon me', however one should be careful and try his best. If something befalls him then he knows that whatever befell him was that which Allaah ordained for him."[16]

Aboo Hafs al-Fallaas, *rahimahullaah*, said: "I said to Yahyaa Ibn Sa'eed during his sickness: "May Allaah give you well being", he answered: 'Whatever is fondest to Allaah is fondest to me.'"[17]

'Abdul-Waahid Ibn Ziyaad, *rahimahullaah*, said: "I don't think of any deeds that are more virtuous than patience except for being pleased [with Allaah and His Pre-Ordainment] and similarly I don't know of a level higher or nobler than being pleased [with Allaah and His Pre-Ordainment] and it is the head of loving Allaah."[18]

---

[14] *As-Sabr* (pg. 31)
[15] *Al-Hilyah* (vol. 4/pg. 56)
[16] *Al-Hilyah* (vol. 2/pg. 202)
[17] *As-Siyar* (vol. 9/pg. 182)
[18] *Al-Hilyah* (vol. 6/pg. 163)

Yoosuf Ibn Asbaat, *rahimahullaah*, said: "I heard Sufyaan ath-Thauree saying: 'Three qualities are from patience: Not to speak about your misfortune or your pain, and don't praise yourself.'"[19]

Qataadah, *rahimahullaah*, said: "Patience from faith is like the hands to the body. Whoever is not patient upon adversity cannot be thankful in prosperity, and if patience was a man he would be handsome and noble."[20]

Narrated Ibn Abee Rawaad, *rahimahullaah*: "Once I saw a sore on Muhammad Ibn Waassi's hand and it was as if he saw how difficult I saw that to be. He asked me: 'Do you know what favor Allaah has over me with regards to this blister?' I kept silent. He continued: 'He didn't make it on my eye, or the tip of my tongue, or the tip of my penis.' Thereupon his sore became easy for me to bear."[21]

Once a man praised Ahnaf Ibn Qays, *rahimahullaah*, saying: 'How patient you are?' He replied: "Impatience is the worst of both situations; it pushes you further away from your goal, brings about regret and remains upon as disgrace."[22]

'Umar Ibn 'Abdil-Azeez, *rahimahullaah*, said: "Allaah never blesses a slave with a favor and then takes away from him and then recompenses him its place with patience, except that which He

---

[19] *Al-Hilyah* (vol. 6/pg. 389)

[20] *As-Sabr* (pg. 163)

[21] *As-Sabr* (pg. 184)

[22] *As-Sabr* (pg. 191)

recompensed him with [the patience] was better than what He took away from him."[23]

Aboo Sa'eed al-Khazzaaz, *rahimahullaah,* said: "Good times and well being hides the pious from the wicked, so when calamity comes the men are made clear [from the boys]."[24]

Narrated Sayyaar, *rahimahullaah:* 'Abdul-Waahid Ibn Ziyaad said: "Whoever intends to be patient upon the truth, Allaah will strengthen him and make him patient. And whoever has firm resolve upon bearing patience from the disobedience to Allaah, He will aid him upon that and protect him from falling into it."[25]

---

[23] *'Iddatus-Saabireen* (pg. 24)

[24] *Sifatus-Safwah* (vol. 2/pg. 438)

[25] *Al-Hilyah* (vol. 3/pg. 183)

Being Cautious From Acts of Disobedience and Hastening Towards Acts of Obedience[26]

Narrated Qaasim, *rahimahullaah*: "Once Ibn 'Abbaas, *radiyAllaahu 'anhumma*, was asked about a man who is diligent in good deeds but commits some sins and about a man who isn't diligent in worship but he doesn't commit sins, so he said: "Safety from sins is more beloved to me."[27]

Anas, *radiyAllaahu 'anhu*, said: Verily, a man could be deprived from standing in prayer at night and fasting during the day because of a lie that he tells."[28]

Ibn-'Abbaas, *radiyAllaahu 'anhumaa*, said: "There cannot be a major sin along with seeking Allaah's forgiveness nor a minor sin while being persistent upon it."[29]

Aboo Ayoob al-Ansaaree, *rahimahullaah*, said: "Indeed, a man will do a good deed and rely on it and perform sins that he sees to be minor until he comes to Allaah and they have ripped him apart, and indeed a man will do a bad deed and be afraid of it so much so that he will go to Allaah in safety."[30]

---

[26] "*Min Akhbaaris-Salaf*" (pg. 185-202) with abridgement and adjustment.

[27] *az-Zuhd* of Aboo Daawood (pg. 337)

[28] *ash-Shu'ab* (vol. 4/pg. 4890)

[29] *ash-Shu'ab* (vol. 5/pg. 7268)

[30] *ash-Shu'ab* (pg. 6880)

Aboo 'Abdir-Rahmaan Ibn Abee Laylaa, *rahimahullaah*, said: "Aboo Dardaa' wrote to the official of Egypt, Maslamah Ibn Makhlad: "Indeed, when the slave performs obedience to Allaah, Allaah will love him and make him beloved to His creature and when he disobeys Allaah, He will hate him and make him hated to the creation."[31]

Aboo Moosaa al-Ash'aree, *radiyAllaahu 'anhu*, was extremely diligent in worship before his death so it was said to him, "If you any refrained from this were a little or were a little gentle with yourself." He replied: "When a horse is sent off to run and it is close to the end of race track it pushes out all that it has and the time that is left from my life is less than that." The reporter said: "So he didn't cease to be upon that state until he died."[32]

'Amr Ibn Maymoon, *rahimahullaah*, said: "My father did not used to make abundant fasting and prayer, however he was never fond of disobeying Allaah."[33]

Ja'far Ibn Muhammad Ibn 'Alee, *rahimahullaah*, said: "Whoever Allaah delivers from the disgrace of disobedience into the might of piety will have been enriched without any wealth, and given power without any kinship, and made him feel at ease without any companion."[34]

---

[31] *az-Zuhd* of Aboo Daawood (pg. 240)
[32] *Qisarul-Amal* (pg. 150)
[33] *al-Hilyah* (vol. 4/pg. 82)
[34] *ash-Shu'ab* (pg. 6849)

Sa'eed Ibn Jubayr, *rahimahullaah,* said: "From wasting money is that
Allaah provides you with lawful sustenance and you spend it in the
disobedience of Allaah."[35]

'Umar Ibn 'Abdil-'Azeez, *rahimahullaah,* said: "Taqwaa is not
standing at night and fasting during the day and mixing other deeds
besides this, rather taqwaa is performing what Allaah has made
obligatory and avoiding what Allaah has made unlawful. So if there
are other deeds along with this, then it is good upon good."[36]

Narrated Mu'tamar Ibn Sulaymaan, *rahimahullaah,* that his father
said: "Indeed, a man commits a sin and wakes up the next morning
wearing its humiliation."[37]

Al-Auzaa'iee, *rahimahullaah,* said: "It used to be said: 'From the
major sins is for a man to do a sin and then look down upon it.'"[38]

Reported Ibn al-Mubaarak, *rahimahullaah:* Once Wuhayb Ibn al-
Ward was asked: "Will the one who disobeys Allaah find the
sweetness of worship?" He replied: 'No, nor the one who even
thinks about disobeying Allaah.'"[39]

Narrated Aboo Haywah, *rahimahullaah:* "Once I entered upon Bakr
Ibn 'Abdillaah al-Muzanee while we were visiting him in his last

---

[35] *al-Hilyah* (vol. 4/pg. 281)

[36] *Jaami'ul 'Uloom wal-Hikam* (pg. 91)

[37] *ash-Shu'ab* (pg. 6839)

[38] *ash-Shu'ab* (pg. 6752)

[39] *ash-Shu'ab* (pg. 833)

sickness so he raised his head and said, 'May Allaah have mercy on a slave that Allaah has provided with physical strength and therefore acted upon Allaah's obedience, or [a slave] whose physical weakness was a cause for him to desist from disobeying Allaah."[40]

Makhool ad-Dimashqee, *rahimahullaah,* said: "Those individuals who make the least sins are those who have the softest hearts."[41]

Bishr Ibn al-Haarith, *rahimahullaah,* said: "You will not find the sweetness of worship until you place a barrier between yourself your lusts."[42]

Yahyaa Ibn Abe Katheer, *rahimahullaah,* said: "It used to be said: 'The slaves cannot honor themselves with something more noble than obeying Allaah, nor can they disgrace themselves with something more ugly than disobeying Allaah, the Mighty and Majestic.'"[43]

Abul-Hasan al-Muzayyan, *rahimahullaah,* said: "A sin committed after another sin is a punishment for the first sin and a good deed that is done after another good deed is the punishment for the first bad deed."[44]

---

[40] *az-Zuhd* (pg. 390)

[41] *az-Zuhd* of Ahmad (pg. 463)

[42] *as-Siyar* (vol.10/pg. 473)

[43] *Muhaasabatun-Nafs* (pg. 97)

[44] *Sifatus-Safwah* (vol. 2/pg. 456)

Ash-Shaafi'ee, *rahimahullaah*, said: "Avoiding sins and leaving off
that which doesn't concern an individual enlightens the heart."[45]

Once one of the people of the past heard Fudayl Ibn 'Iyaad,
rahimahullaah, saying in the Masjid al-Haraam: "The poorer I am,
the more righteous I am, and when I commit an act of disobedience
to Allaah I can see the effects of that in how my donkey and how my
guard acts towards me."[46]

Once Yahyaa Ibn Mu'aadh, *rahimahullaah*, saw a man digging at a
mountain on a very hot day so he said: "The son of Aadam is truly
miskeen! Breaking apart boulders is easier upon him them leaving off
sins."[47]

Salamah Ibn Deenaar, *rahimahullaah*, said: "When you see Allaah
continually blessing you and you are disobeying Him then
beware!"[48]

Bakr Ibn 'Abdillaah al-Muzanee, *rahimahullaah*, said: "Whoever
commits a sin laughing will enter the Fire crying."[49]

Al-Qaadee 'Iyaad, *rahimahullaah*, said: "According to how small you
look at the sin is how great it will be in the sight of Allaah and

---

[45] *as-Siyar* (vol. 10/pg. 98)
[46] *al-Hilyah* (vol. 8/pg. 109)
[47] *as-Siyar* (vol. 13/pg. 15)
[48] *Sifatus-Safwah* (vol. 2/pg. 157)
[49] *al-Hilyah* (vol. 6/pg. 185)

according to how greatly you look at the sin the smaller it will be in the sight of Allaah."[50]

Narrated al-Auzaa'iee, *rahimahullaah,*: "Once I heard Bilaal Ibn Sa'd saying: 'Do not look how small the sin is but instead look at how great is the One that you have disobeyed."[51]

Narrated 'Ataa' Ibn as-Saa'id, *rahimahullaah:* "We entered upon Aboo 'Abdir-Rahmaan as-Sulamee visiting him and some people began to encourage him to have hope for Allaah, thereupon he said: "How can I not hope for my Lord and I have fasted over eighty ramadans?!!',"[52]

Narrated al-Mu'tamir, *rahimahullaah,* from his father: "The good deed is light in the heart and strength upon performing good deeds and the bad deed is darkness in the heart and weakness upon performing good deeds."[53]

Wahb Ibn Munabbih, *rahimahullaah,* said: "Whoever tries to perform worship he will increase in strength and whoever acts lazily he will increase in lethargy."[54]

---

[50] *as-Siyar* (vol. 8/pg. 428)

[51] *al-Hilyah* (vol. 5/pg. 223)

[52] *al-Muhtadareen* (pg. 206)

[53] *al-Hilyah* (vol. 3/pg. 30)

[54] *az-Zuhd* of Ahmad (pg. 477)

Aboo Haazim Salamah Ibn Deenaar, *rahimahullaah,* said: "Look at every act that you would hate to die while committing, and then abandon it."[55]

Narrated Ahmad Ibn Salamah, *rahimahullaah:* "Once Hannaad Ibn as-Saree finished narrating to us some ahaadeeth so he offered wudoo, went to the masjid and stayed there until noon and then returned to his house and I was with him. He came and led us in the *Dhur* prayer, then stood up and began to offer voluntary prayer until 'Asr and crying abundantly. Then he led us in the 'Asr prayer and began to read from the *Mushaf* until the time of the *Maghrib* prayer. Some of his neighbors said: "Look how patient he is upon worship. He replied: 'This has been his worship in the daytime for seventy years, so what would be the case if you saw his worship at night."[56]

Khaalid Ibn Ma'daan, *rahimahullaah,* said: "When a door leading to good is opened up for one of you then he should hasten to it because you don't know when it will be shut."[57]

Qa'qaa' Ibn Hakeem, *rahimahullaah,* said: "I have prepared for death over thirty years ago; if it came to me I wouldn't like to delay anything."[58]

---

[55] *al-Musannaf* (vol. 7/pg. 194)
[56] *as-Siyar* (vol. 11/pg. 466)
[57] *al-Hilyah* (vol. 5/pg. 211)
[58] *Qisarul-Aml* (pg. 178)

Narrated al-Firyaabee, *rahimahullaah*: "Sufyaan at-Thauree used to offer prayer and then turn towards the youth and say: 'If you don't offer prayer today then when?'"[59]

Repentance and Seeking Allaah's Forgiveness[60]

Yoonus Ibn Khabbaab, *rahimahullaah*, said: "Once Mujaahid said to me, and he was a true brother to me indeed, 'Should I not inform you of whom the one who is the oft-returner to Allaah in repentance and he who preserves his covenant with Allaah is?' I replied: "Of course" He said: 'He is the man who remembers his sins when he secludes himself and seeks forgiveness for them.'"[61]

Ahmad Ibn 'Aasim, *rahimahullaah*, said: "Surely, this is the easy prey, clean up the rest of your life and you will be forgiven for your past."[62]

Talq Ibn Habeeb, *rahimahullaah*, said: "Verily, Allaah's rights are far too heavy for the slaves to fulfill, and indeed, the favors of Allaah are far too many for the slaves to count, however, wake up as repentants and go to sleep as repentants."[63]

On the authority of Ja'far, *rahimahullaah*, who reported: Once it was said to Sa'eed Ibn Jubayr: 'Who from the people is of the most worship?' He answered: "The man who has committed sins and whenever he remembers his sins he looks down on his [good] deeds."[64]

---

[60] *Min Akhbaaris-Salaf* (pg. 90-92) with adbridgment and adjustment

[61] *Az-Zuhd* of Ahmad (pg. 452)

[62] *Az-Zuhd al-Kabeer* (pg. 228)

[63] *Al-Musannaf* (vol. 7/pg. 182)

[64] *Sifatus-Safwah* (vol. 2/pg. 665)

Abul-Maleeh, *rahimahullaah,* said: "Once I heard Maymoon Ibn Mihraan saying: 'There isn't any good in the *Dunyaa* except two men: a man who is a repentant and a man who strives hard for the stations [in the Hereafter].'"[65]

'Aun Ibn 'Abdillaah, *rahimahullaah,* said: "Sit in the company of those who make constant repentance for indeed, they have softest hearts from amongst the people."[66]

'Aun Ibn 'Abdillaah Ibn 'Utbah, *rahimahullaah,* said: "The slave worrying about his sins is a motive to leaving them off, his remorse for them is a key to repentance, and a slave will not continue to worry about the sin that he commits until it becomes more beneficial to him then some of his good deeds."[67]

Hasan [al-Basree], *rahimahullaah,* said: "Verily, a man commits a sin and never forgets it and he won't cease to be afraid from it until he enters Paradise."[68]

Narrated Maalik Ibn Mighwal, *rahimahullaah:* "I heard Aboo Yahyaa complaining to Mujaahid about sins so he asked him, 'Where are you from the eraser?' Meaning *al-Istighfaar* [seeking Allaah's forgiveness]."[69]

---

[65] *Al-Hilyah* (vol. 4/pg. 83)
[66] *Al-Hilyah* (vol. 4/pg. 249)
[67] *Al-Hilyah* (vol. 4/pg. 251)
[68] *Az-Zuhd* of Ahmad (pg. 338)
[69] *Az-Zuhd* of Ahmad (pg. 455)

Abul-Minhaal, *rahimahullaah,* said: "There can't possibly a better neighbor for the slave in his grave then abundant *istighfaar.*"[70]

'Abdullaah Ibn Shaqeeq, *rahimahullaah,* said: "The men are three: A man who performed a good deed so he hopes for its reward, a man who performed a bad deed and then repented so he hopes for Allaah's forgiveness, and a man who is a liar and persists upon sins and says: 'I hope for Allaah's forgiveness'. Whoever knows himself to be a bad doer then his fear should out weigh his hope."[71]

---

[70] *Az-Zuhd* of Ahmad (pg. 396)
[71] *Ash-Shu'ab* (vol. 2/pg. 1016)

Invoking Allaah and Supplicating to Him, the Exalted[72]

Abud-Dardaa', *rahimahullaah*, said: "Whoever knocks on the door then it is on the brink of it being opened up for him, and whoever makes a lot of *du'aa* then his supplication is on the verge of being answered."[73]

'Aaishah, *radiyAllahu 'anhaa*, said: "Ask Allaah to facilitate everything, even the thong to your sandal, for if Allaah had not made facilitation, it would not be facilitated."[74]

Wahb Ibn Munabbih, *rahimahullaah*, said: "Whoever is pleased with his supplication being answered then let him eat from fine, lawful means."[75]

Taawoos, *rahimahullaah*, said: "Being truthful suffices *du'aa* just as salt suffices the food."[76]

On the authority of Muhammad Ibn al-Waleed, *rahimahullaah*, who reported: Once 'Umar Ibn 'Abdil-'Azeez passed by a man in whose hand were stones he played with and at the time he was supplicating, 'O Allah! Allow me to marry one of the *Hoor al-'Eeen* [virgin maidens of Paradise]', so 'Umar turned to him and cried out:

---

[72] Min Akhbaaris-Salaf with adbrigment and adjustment (pg. 92-93)

[73] Ash-Shu'ab (vol. 2/pg. 1142)

[74] Ash-Shu'ab (vol. 2/pg. 1142)

[75] Jaami'ul-'Uloom wal-Hikam (pg. 50)

[76] Ash-Shu'ab (pg. 1110)

"What an evil proposer you are! Certainly you should throw these stones and make your *du'aa* sincere and pure to Allaah."[77]

Al-Auzaa'iee, *rahimahullaah,* said: "The most excellent *du'aa* is insistence upon Allaah and earnest imploring unto Him."[78]

Ibn 'Uyaynah, *rahimahullaah,* said: "Don't ever leave off making *du'aa* nor allow what [bad deeds] you commit to prevent you from it, for indeed Allaah answered the *du'aa* of Iblees and he is the most evil of creation [when he said to Allaah]: {He (Iblees) said: *"Grant me respite until the Day in which they will be resurrected." He (Allaah, the Exalted) said: "Indeed, you are from those who are granted respite." [Soorah al-A'raf (7): 14-15]*[79]

Narrated Thaabit, *rahimahullaah:* "We used to sit with Aboo 'Uthmaan an-Nahdee and he would remind us, to make *du'aa* and then say: 'Indeed this *du'aa* has been answered and we have been forgiven.' Then he would keep silent shortly and say: 'If we are truthful.'"[80]

Aboo Ja'far Muhammad Ibn 'Alee, *rahimahullaah,* said: "There isn't anything more beloved to Allaah, the Mighty and Majestic, than for Him to be asked. Nothing repels the Pre-Ordainment except for

---

[77] *Al-HIlyah* (vol. 5/pg. 287)
[78] *Ash-Shu'ab* (vol. 2/pg. 1107)
[79] *Ash-Shu'ab* (vol. 2/pg. 1147)
[80] *Az-Zuhd of Ahmad* (pg. 380)

du'aa. The good that has the swiftest reward is benevolence and the evil that has the swiftest punishment is aggression. It is a sufficient portion of defect for a person to clearly see from the people [of mistakes and shortcomings] that which he is blind of from his own self, for him to enjoin the people with that which he isn't able to abandon and or to annoy his companion with that which doesn't concern him."[81]

Yahyaa Ibn Mu'aadh, *rahimahullaah,* said: "Do not find slow the answer to your *du'aas* when you have shut off its path with your sins."[82]

---

[81] *Al-Hilyah* (vol. 3/pg. 188)
[82] *As-Siyar* (vol. 13/pg. 15)

Reading the Qur'aan and Reflecting upon its Meanings[83]

'Abdullaah Ibn Mas'ood, *radiyAllaahu 'anhu*, said: "Verily, these hearts are vessels, so fill them up with the Qur'aan and do not fill them up with anything else besides it."[84]

Ibn 'Abbaas, *radiyAllaahu 'anhumaa*, said: "Allaah has guaranteed for the one who follows the Qur'aan that he won't go astray in worldly life nor be miserable in the Hereafter." Then he recited: *"So whoever follows my guidance will neither go astray nor be miserable [Soorah Ta-Ha (20): 123]*[85]

On the authority Naafi' who reported that Ibn 'Umar, *radiyAllaahu 'anhumaa*, used to recite in his prayer and pass by a verse in which Paradise is mentioned so he would stop and ask Allaah for Paradise, supplicate and cry. He would also pass by a verse in which the Fire is mentioned so he would stop, supplicate and seek the forgiveness of Allaah, the Mighty and Majestic.[86]

'Abdullaah [Ibn Mas'ood], *radiyAllahu 'anhu,* said: "Recite the Qur'aan in seven days but do not recite it in less than three days and a man should strictly guard his daily recitation of one *juz*."[87]

---

[83] *Min Akhbaaris-Salaf* with adbrigment and adjustment (pg. 100-109)
[84] *Al-Musannaf* (vol. 7/pg. 106)
[85] *Al-Musannaf* (vol. 7/pg. 136)
[86] *Az-Zuhd* of Ahmad (pg. 241)
[87] *Ash-Shu'ab* (vol. 2/pg. 2173)

Ibn Mas'ood, *radiyAllahu 'anhu*, said: "Constantly look into the *Mushaf*."[88]

Reported Yoonus Ibn Jubayr, *rahimahullaah*: "We accompanied Jundub until we reached the *makaatib* citadel and asked him to give us advice. He answered: 'I advice you with the *taqwaa* of Allaah and I enjoin you with the Qur'aan for indeed it is the light for a dark night and the illumination of the day."[89]

Narrated Farwah Ibn Naufal, *rahimahullaah*: "Once I was with Khabbaab, *radiyAllaahu 'anhu*, so we went out to the masjid and he grabbed my hand and said to me: "Seek nearness unto Allaah to the best of your ability for surely, you cannot get close to Him with something more beloved to Him than His speech."[90]

On the authority of 'Abdullaah Ibn 'Urwah, *rahimahullaah*, who said: "I asked my grandmother Asmaa, "How were the Companions of the Prophet, *sallAllahu 'alayhi wa sallam*, when they recited the Qur'aan?" She replied, 'Their eyes watered and their skins trembled just as Allaah has described them [in the Qur'aan]'."[91]

Ash-Sha'bee, *rahimahullaah*, said: "When you recite the Qur'aan then make your heart understand it and allow your ears to hear it."[92]

---

[88] *Ash-Shu'ab* (pg. 2028)
[89] *Ash-Shu'ab* (pg. 1873)
[90] *Ash-Shu'ab* (pg. 1463)
[91] *Ash-Shu'ab* (pg. 1900)
[92] *Ash-Shu'ab* (pg. 1927)

'Amr Ibn Murrah, *rahimahullaah*, said: "I dislike to pass by a parable in the Qur'aan and I don't know it, because Allaah, the Exalted, says: ***"And those are the parables that we make, and none can truly understand them but those who have knowledge."*** *[Soorah Al-'Ankabut (29):43]*[93]

Stated Sufyaan Ibn 'Uyaynah, *rahimahullaah*: "By Allaah! You will never reach the apex of this affair until nothing is more beloved to you than Allah, the Mighty and Majestic, and whoever loves the Qur'aan will indeed love Allaah, the Mighty and Majestic."[94]

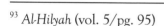

---

[93] *Al-Hilyah* (vol. 5/pg. 95)
[94] *Ash-Shu'ab* (vol. 1/pg. 407)

The Prayer and Offering an Abundance of it[95]

'Abdullaah Ibn Mas'ood, *radiyAllaahu 'anhu*: "The one who offers the
prayer knocks on the door and whoever constantly knocks on the
king's door is on the brink of having it opened up for him."[96]

Stated Hudhayfah, *radiyAllaahu 'anhu*: "There isn't a time that
Allaah, the Mighty and Majestic, lauds the slave more than the time
in which He finds His [the slave's] face dirty [from sujood]."[97]

Bakr Ibn 'Abdillaah al-Muzanee, *rahimahullaah*, said: "Who is similar
to you o son of Aadam? The path between you, water and the
mihraab is left open, whenever you please you can purify yourself
and enter upon your Lord, the Mighty and Majestic, without any
translator or screen."[98]

Narrated al-Auzaa'iee, *rahimahullaah*: 'Umar Ibn 'Abdil-Azeez wrote
to his governors: 'Avoid tasks at the time of the prayer, for surely,
whoever wastes it [the prayer] will waste the other obligations of
Islaam even more."[99]

---

[95] *Min Akhbaaris-Salaf* with adbrigment and adjustment (pg. 50-54)
[96] *Az-Zuhd* of Ahmad pg. 153
[97] *Az-Zuhd* of Ahmad (pg. 224)
[98] *Al-Bidaayah wan-Nihaayah* (vol. 9/pg. 256)
[99] *Al-Hilyah* (vol. 5/pg. 316)

Reported Hasan Ibn Najeeh ar-Raqaashee, *rahimahullaah*: "I heard
Hasan al-Basree saying: 'O son of Aadam! What can possibly be
costly to you from your deen if the prayer has become something
light to you?'"[100]

Narrated Muslim al-Makkee, *rahimahullaah*: "Once I saw Ibn az-
Zubayr go into *rukoo'* so I read soorah al-Baqarah, Aali 'Imraan, an-
Nisaa' and al-Maa'idah and he did not raise his head."[101]

Reported Aboo Qatn, *rahimahullaah*: "I never saw Shu'bah making
rukoo' except that I thought he forgot nor have I ever saw him sitting
between the two prostrations except that I thought that he
forgot."[102]

Narrated Ibn Wahb, *rahimahullaah*: "Once I saw ath-Thauree in the
Haram after *maghrib* offering voluntary prayer. Then he went down
into sujood and he didn't raise his head until the *adhaan* for 'ishaa
was made."[103]

Reported 'Abdaan, *rahimahullaah*: "Hudbah Ibn Hakeem used to
make *tasbeeh* in *rukoo'* and *sujood* more than thirty times."[104]

---

[100] *At-Tahajjud wa Qiyaamul-Layl* (pg. 288)

[101] *Az-Zuhd* of Aboo Daawood (pg. 348)

[102] *As-Siyar* (vol. 7/pg. 207)

[103] *As-Siyar* (vol. 7/pg. 296)

[104] *As-Siyar* (vol. 11/pg. 99)

Narrated 'Alaa, *rahimahullaah*: "Once I came to the masjid of Waasit and the *mu'adhin* made the *adhaan* for *dhur*. Afterwards Mansoor Ibn Zaadhaan came and began offering prayer. I saw that he made *sujood* eleven times before the *iqaamah* was made for the prayer."[105]

Some of the Students of Abush-Shaykh reported that they never entered upon Abush-Shaykh except that he was offering prayer.[106]

Reported Ahmad Ibn 'Atiyyah, *rahimahullaah*: "The daily portion of voluntary units for prayer that Muhammad Ibn Samaa'ah made was two hundred units."[107]

Narrated Haarith al-Ghanawee, *rahimahullaah*: "Murrah al-Hamdaanee used to make so much *sujood* that the dirt began to eat away at his forehead. So when he died one of his relatives saw him in a dream in which his forehead was like a brilliant, sparkling star. He asked him, 'What is this that I see with your face?' He replied, 'The place on my forehead that was beginning to get eaten up by dirt has been draped with light.'"[108]

Reported 'Ataa, *rahimahullaah*: "Murrah used to offer six hundred units of voluntary prayer daily and I saw his place of prayer in his house and it was like the kneeling place of a camel."[109]

---

[105] *Al-Hilyah* (vol. 3/pg. 58)
[106] *As-Siyar* (vol. 16/pg. 278)
[107] *As-Siyar* (vol. 10/pg. 646)
[108] *Sifatus-Safwah* (vol. 2/pg. 639)
[109] *As-Siyar* (vol. 4/pg. 75)

Narrated Qays Ibn Rabee', *rahimahullaah*: "I saw Yazeed Ibn Zuray' in a dream and asked him, 'What has Allaah done with you?' He replied, 'I have been granted entrance into Paradise', I then asked, 'Why?' He answered, 'By abundantly offering prayer.'"[110]

Muhaarib, *rahimahullaah*, said: "We accompanied Qaasim Ibn 'Abdir-Rahmaan and he became superior over us with long silence, generosity and abundant prayer."[111]

Stated Masrooq, *rahimahullaah*: "There isn't a time that we wake up or go sleep and I feel remorse upon anything from the worldly life except for not making more *sujood* to Allaah."[112]

Reported 'Ubaydullaah Ibn Sulaymaan Ibn Mu'aawiyah ash-Shaamee, *rahimahullaah*: "Our grandfather wore out two prayer rugs and began on a third with the place of his knees, face and hands from the abundance of prayer that he offered."[113]

Ahmad Ibn Sinaan, *rahimahullaah*, said: "Yazeed and Hushaym were both well known for offering lengthy prayers at night and (during) the day."[114]

❀ ❀ ❀

---

[110] *As-Siyar* (vol. 8/pg. 297)
[111] *As-Samt* (pg. 618)
[112] *Ash-Shu'ab* (pg. 2909)
[113] *As-Siyar* (vol. 7/pg. 398)
[114] *As-Siyar* (vol. 9/pg. 361)

Brotherhood for Allaah's Sake and the Etiquettes of Loving Each Other[115]

Ibn Mas'ood, radiyAllaahu 'anhu, said: "There wouldn't be any sin upon you if you only accompanied the one who aides you upon the remembrance of Allaah."[116]

Stated Mujaahid, rahimahullaah: "I accompanied Ibn 'Umar, radiyAllaahu 'anhumma, with the intention of serving him, but instead it turned out that he was the one who served me."[117]

Stated Aboo Waa'il, rahimahullaah: "Me and my brother went to Rabee' Ibn Khuthaym and he was sitting in the masjid, so he asked us, 'Why have you come?' We responded: 'We have come in order that you may remember Allaah so we can do the same with you, and that you praise Allaah and we may do the same with you', thereupon he raised his hands and said: "All praises are for Allaah that you didn't say: 'We came so that you can drink intoxicants and we can do the same with you, or we came in order that you can commit fornication and we may do the same with you',"[118]

Stated Hasan, rahimahullaah: "The Believer is the mirror of his brother, if he sees something that he is not pleased with, he

---

[115] Min Akhbaaris-Salaf with adbrigment and adjustment (pg. 231-238)

[116] az-Zuhd of Aboo Daawood pg. 146

[117] Makaarimul-Akhlaaq pg. 71

[118] al-Musannaf vol. 7/pg. 146

straightens it out and adjusts it, and protects his honor in private and public."[119]

Once Muhammad Ibn Waasi', *rahimahullaah,* was asked: "What is the most excellent deed in the worldly life?" He responded: "Accompanying your friends and talking with your brothers as long as they befriend each other upon righteousness and piety."[120]

Al-Auzaa'iee, *rahimahullaah,* said: "The friend is like a patch in the garment; if it doesn't resemble the rest of the garment it will make it ugly."[121]

'Abdullaah Ibn Muhammad Ibn Manaazil, *rahimahullaah,* stated: "The Believer seeks excuses for his brothers, and the hypocrite seeks the mistakes for his brothers."[122]

Bishr Ibn al-Haarith, *rahimahullaah,* said: "Look at the person who has the most piety, chastity and purest earning from the people and then accompany him and do not sit with the one who will not help you upon your life in the hereafter."[123]

Stated Ibn Jurayj, *rahimahullaah:* "When you meet your brother then don't ask him, 'From where are you coming?' For perhaps he could be coming from a place that he doesn't like you to know about. So

---

[119] *al- Ikhwaan* of Ibn Abid-Dunyaa pg. 55

[120] *al-Ikhwaan* pg. 50

[121] *ash-Shu'ab* vol. 7/ pg. 9452

[122] *ash-Shu'ab* vol. 7/pg. 11197

[123] *ash-Shu'ab* pg. 9059

if he tells you then you have exposed him, and if he tells you that he came from a place that he didn't, then a lie will be written upon him."[124]

Many of the Salaf used to make a condition on their friends while travelling to serve them, so that they could take advantage of receiving the reward. From them were 'Aamir Ibn Qays and 'Amr Ibn 'Utbah Ibn Farqad, along with their diligence in their own personal worship. Similarly Ibraaheem Ibn Adham used to make a condition upon his friends that whenever they travelled, he would be the only one who called the *adhaan* and served everyone."[125]

Katheer Ibn Sayfee, *rahimahullaah*, said: "Meeting your beloved friends eases stress."[126]

Narrated Hasan Ibn Katheer, *rahimahullaah*: "I complained to Muhammad Ibn 'Alee a need of mine and how my brothers don't look after me, so he said; 'What an evil brother is he who pays you attention when you are wealthy and cuts you off when you are poor' Then he gave orders to his young man servant so he brought a sack of money that amounted seven hundred *dirhams* and said to me: 'Spend all of this, and when it runs out let me know.'"[127]

Narrated Mansoor, *rahimahullaah*: "Once a man said to Hasan al-Basree: 'A man slaughters a sheep, places it down and then invites a

---

[124] *ash-Shu'ab* pg. 10697
[125] *Lataa'if al-Ma'aarif* pg. 413
[126] *al-Ikhwaan* pg. 94
[127] *al-Ikhwaan* pg. 179

group of his brothers to eat it'....He [Hasan] said: 'Where are the likes of these people? These people have all gone away!'"[128]

Stated Yazeed Ibn Abe Ziyaad, *rahimahullaah*: "I never entered upon 'Abdur-Rahmaan Ibn Abee Laylaa except that he narrated to me a good hadeeth and fed me good food."[129]

'Alaa Ibn Musayyib, *rahimahullaah*, said: "Khaytham used to place bags of money in the masjid and sit, so if he saw one of his friends wearing raggedy clothing he would give him a bag of money."[130]

Stated 'Uthmaan Ibn Hakeem, *rahimahullaah*: "Befriend the one who is above you in the religion and below you in the worldly life."[131]

Aboo 'Amr al-'Aufee, *rahimahullaah*, said: "It used to be said: 'Befriend the one, who when you accompany him he will adorn you, when you serve him he will protect your honor, if poverty befalls you he will sustain you, if he sees a good deed from you he counts it and if he sees a mishap from you he covers it, if you speak he believes you and if you make an onslaught he directs you'."[132]

Stated Bakr Ibn 'Abdillaah al-Muzanee, *rahimahullaah*: "Treat your brothers well despite the shortcomings that they have just as you like

---

[128] *al-Ikhwaan* pg. 204

[129] *al-Ikhwaan* pg. 207

[130] *al-Ikhwaan* pg. 224

[131] *as-Samt* of Ibn Abid-Dunyaa pg. 45

[132] *as-Samt* pg. 44

for them to treat you despite the shortcomings that you have. Everyone that you see making a mistake or mishap should not fall from your sight, for surely you are most deserving of this yourself. If you make abundant prayer then don't become conceited, because perhaps the man who wears a garment dyed with saffron or he who drinks fermented dates sometimes keeps his promise more than you. If you keep your promise, don't become conceited and amazed with yourself for indeed the one that you dislike sometimes could possibly keep better relations with his relatives than you. If you keep good relations with your relatives, don't get deceived and amazed for indeed perhaps the one who you dislike sometimes could fast more than you do."[133]

Yahyaa Ibn Abee Katheer, *rahimahullaah*, said: "The best of brothers are those who say: "Come! Let's fast before we die, and the worst of brothers are those who say, 'Come let's eat and drink before we die'."[134]

Stated Ja'far Ibn Burqaan, *rahimahullaah*: "Maymoon Ibn Mihraan said to me: 'O Ja'far! Say something to me in my face that I dislike, for surely a man cannot give his brother sincere advice until he says something that he dislikes to his face'."[135]

---

[133] *at-Taubeekh* of Abush-Shaykh pg. 54

[134] *al-Hilyah* vol. 3/pg. 71

[135] *al-Hilyah* vol. 4/pg. 86

Fudayl Ibn 'Iyaad, *rahimahullaah,* said: "Whoever seeks a brother without any faults would never have a brother to be his friend."[136]

Stated Hubayrah, *rahimahullaah:* "Consider the people based upon their friends."[137]

---

[136] *Raudatul-'Uqalaa* pg. 169
[137] *Raudatul-'Uqalaa* pg. 108

Thinking About Death and the Hereafter[138]

Anas, *radiyAllaahu 'anhu*, said: "I shall inform you of two days of
which the creation has not heard of the likes of them: "The day in
which the bearer of glad tidings comes to you from Allaah, either
with pleasure or abhorrence, and a day in which you will stand in
fear receiving your book either in your right hand or your left
hand."[139]

Stated Mu'aadh, *radiyAllaahu 'anhu*: "One day Aboo Bakr,
radiyAllaahu 'anhu, entered a garden and there was a finch standing
in the shade of a tree, so he sighed deeply and then said: "Glad
tidings to you o bird! You eat fruit, receive shade from the trees and
then you pass on to no reckoning; only if Aboo Bakr was like
you!"[140]

Narrated Haani', the freed slave of 'Uthmaan: "Whenever
'Uthmaan, *radiyAllaahu 'anhu*, used to stand over a grave, his beard
would become wet from tears."[141]

'Abdullaah Ibn Mas'ood said: "There isn't any true relaxation for
the Believers besides the meeting of Allaah."[142]

---

[138] *Min Akhbaaris-Salaf* (pg. 212-221)

[139] *az-Zuhd* of Aboo Daawood pg. 343

[140] *al-Mutamanniyeen* pg. 71

[141] *al-Hilyah* vol. 1/pg. 61

[142] *az-Zuhd* of Ahmad pg. 194.

Stated Bilaal Ibn Sa'd, *rahimahullaah*: "Perhaps a happy person is in total fraud, he eats, drinks and laughs, and it has already been proven true in the register of Allaah [i.e. the Pre Decree] that he will be from the fuel of the fire!"[143]

Stated Ahmad Ibn Harb, *rahimahullaah*: "Verily one of us prefers shade over standing in the sun, but he won't prefer Paradise over the Fire!"[144]

Maalik Ibn Deenaar, *rahimahullaah*, said: "By Allaah! If it was possible for me not to sleep, I would not sleep out of fear that the punishment would descend and I am asleep. By Allaah! If I had some helpers, I would spread them out among the *Dunyaa* and give them orders to cry out to the people, 'O mankind! The Fire! The Fire!'"[145]

Rabee' Ibn Khuthaym, *rahimahullaah*, said: "Make abundant mention of this death, the likes of which you have not tasted before."[146]

Narrated Qabeesah, *rahimahullaah*: "I have never sat with Sufyaan except that I thought about death, and I have not seen anyone who thought about it more than him."[147]

---

[143] *Sifatus-Safwah* vol. 4/pg. 218

[144] *al-Ihyaa* vol. 4/pg. 568

[145] *al-Ihyaa* vol. 4/pg. 567

[146] *al-Hilyah* vol. 2/pg. 114

[147] *as-Siyar* vol. 7/pg. 240

Narrated 'Abdullaah as-Sindee, *rahimahullaah*: Mubaarak wrote to his brother Sufyaan complaining about him going blind, so he wrote back to him saying: "O my brother! I have understood your letter in which you complained to your Lord. Think about death and losing your eyesight will be lesser on you."[148]

Ibn as-Sammaak, *rahimahullaah* said: "The aspiration of the intellectual is salvation and fleeing, and the goal of the idiot is play and amusement. Quite strange is the eye that finds pleasure in slumber, and the angle of death is with it on the pillow. Will it then be anyone who is wide awakens from his sleep?! Will it then be anyone who comes out of his gets up out of his?! Why wouldn't you invest in your hereafter for your own self?"[149]

Stated Hasan al-Basree, *rahimahullaah*: "What do you think about a day in which they [all of mankind] have stood on their feet for a period of time that amounts fifty thousand years, they haven't eaten any food, nor drank any drink, until the point that their throats have become severed out of thirst and their insides burnt upon out of hunger, and then they will be taken to the Fire and given drink from a scorching, hot spring?!!"[150]

Ibraaheem Ibn Ad'ham, *rahimahullaah*, said: "Indeed death has a standing that no one can bear to swallow except a man of fear and obedience who was expecting it. So whoever is obedient then he will have life, honor and salvation from the punishment of the fire.

---

[148] *al-Hilyah* vol. 7/pg. 22
[149] *al-Ihyaa* vol. 4/pg. 500
[150] *al-Ihyaa* vol. 4/pg. 500

Whoever is sinful then he will be between regret and sorrow on the
Day of Horrid Tragedy and Catastrophe."[151]

Stated Mutarrif Ibn 'Abdillaah, *rahimahullaah*: "Verily, this death
has certainly corrupted upon the people of pleasure their pleasure,
so seek pleasure in which there is no death."[152]

Narrated Mubaarak Ibn Fadaalah, *rahimahullaah*: "I heard Hasan al-
Basree saying: 'O Son of Aadam! Walk on earth with your feet as
long as you wish, for it shall soon be your grave. You have not
ceased to subtract from your life span since you came from your
mothers' womb.'"[153]

Once Muhammad Ibn Waasi', *rahimahullaah*, was asked how he felt
when waking up? He responded: "What do you think about a man,
who each day travels a closer distance to the Hereafter."[154]

Once 'Alaa Ibn Muhammad, *rahimahullaah*, entered upon 'Ataa as-
Sulaymee, *rahimahullaah*, and he had passed out so he asked his wife
Umm Ja'far, *rahimahallaah*, "What is the matter with 'Ataa? She
replied: Our neighbor lit her clay oven so he looked towards it
thereupon he passed out."[155]

---

[151] *al-Hilyah* vol. 8/pg. 13

[152] *Lataa'if al-Ma'aarif* pg. 70

[153] *al-Hilyah* vol. 2/pg. 155

[154] *al-Hilyah* vol. 2/pg. 348

[155] *Tadhkiratul-Huffaadh* vol. 1/pg. 216

Once a meal was presented to Rabaah' al-Qaysee, *rahimahullaah,* so he ate from it and someone said to him, "Eat more, because I don't see that you have become full." He responded to him: "How can I become full during the days of the worldly life and the Tree of *Zaqqoom* which will be the food of the sinful lies ahead of me?!" The food was taken from in front of him and he said: "You are upon something and we are upon something else."[156]

Narrated Daawood Ibn al-Muhabbir, *rahimahullaah* from his father who said: "Once Rabee' Ibn Badr, *rahimahullaah,* passed by us and we were preparing a shroud for a deceased man, so he asked: 'Who is this stranger with you?' We replied: 'He is not a stranger; instead he was a close loved one to us.' He said: 'So he began to cry and said: 'And who is more strange than a dead man amongst the living?!!' Thereupon all of them began to cry."[157]

Narrated Muslim Ibn Ibraaheem, *rahimahullaah:* "Hishaam ad-Dastawaa'iee, *rahimahullaah,* never used to put out his lamp at night until the morning and used to say: 'Whenever I see the darkness, I think about the darkness of the grave.'"[158]

Bishr Ibn Mansoor, *rahimahullaah,* said: "Verily, I think of something from the affairs of the worldly life which distracts me from thinking about the Hereafter, and I fear upon my sanity."[159]

❀ ❀ ❀

---

[156] *Jaami'ul-'Uloom* pg. 426

[157] *al-Hilyah* vol. 6/pg. 297

[158] *al-Hilyah* vol. 6/pg. 221

[159] *al-Hilyah* vol. 6/pg. 241

Preserving One's Time[160]

'Abdullaah Ibn Mas'ood, *radiyAllaahu 'anhu*, said: "Indeed, I hate to
see a man totally free, not doing anything from the work of the life
of this world nor the Hereafter."[161]

Stated Aboo Hurayrah, *radiyAllaahu 'anhu*: "Make performing good
deeds your normal practice for surely, performing good deeds can
become a habit, but beware of the habit of the procrastinator."[162]

Hasan al-Basre, *rahimahullaah*, said: "O assembly of Muslims! Beware
of procrastination, [saying] 'I'll do this, I'll do that',"[163]

Narrated 'Abdul-Waahid Ibn Safwaan, *rahimahullaah*: "Once we
were with Hasan in a funeral so he said: May Allaah have mercy on
a man who works deeds for the like of this day. For surely, today you
have the ability to work deeds the likes of which your brothers in
these graves don't, so take advantage of good health and free time
before the great terror and reckoning comes."[164]

Sufyaan ath-Thauree, *rahimahullaah*, said: "Whoever is fond of the
thighs of women will never succeed."[165]

---

[160] *Min Akhbaaris-Salaf* (pg. 277-281) with slight adjustment.

[161] *al-Hilyah* vol. 1/pg. 130

[162] *Qisarul-Aml* pg. 215

[163] *Qisarul-Aml* pg. 212

[164] *Qisarul-Aml* pg.141

[165] *al-Hilyah* vol. 7/pg. 12

Stated Aboo Bakr Ibn 'Ayyaash, *rahimahullaah*: "If a *dirham* fell and
got lost from one of them, he would spend his entire day saying,
'Verily to Allaah we belong, my *dirham* is lost!' But he wouldn't say:
'My day has gone by and I haven't accomplished anything!'"[166]

Aboo Muslim al-Khaulaanee, *rahimahullaah*, used to say: "If I saw
Paradise or the Fire in an eye's view today, I wouldn't have anything
extra to put forth."[167]

Once, one of the Salaf gave his friends some advice saying: "When
you leave me then split up; so perhaps one of you will read some
Qur'aan in the road, because whenever you meet up with each you
talk."[168]

'Ubayd Ibn Ya'eesh, *rahimahullaah*, said: "For thirty years I have not
eaten with my hands; my sister would feed me while I wrote down
ahaadeeth!"[169]

Stated Yahyaa Ibn al-Qaasim, *rahimahullaah*: "Ibn Sakeenah,
rahimahullaah, used to be a scholar with vast knowledge. He never
wasted any of his time; whenever we entered upon him he would say
to us: 'Don't say anything more than the salaams and (ask about
the) issue of such and such...' because of his great diligence upon

---

[166] *al-Hilyah* vol. 8pg. 303

[167] *as-Siyar* vol. 4/pg. 9

[168] *Saydul-Khaatir* pg. 480

[169] *al-Jaami' li Akhlaaqir-Raawee wa Aadaabis-Saami'* vol. 2/pg. 178

researching and establishing the rulings and regulations of the
Religion."[170]

Sulaymaan at-Taymee, *rahimahullaah*, said: "We never came to
Hammaad Ibn Salamah during any time that Allaah could be
obeyed and worshipped in except that we found him obeying
Allaah. If it was a time for prayer we found him offering prayer, if it
wasn't a time of prayer we found him either making *wudoo*, visiting a
sick person, carrying a *janaazah*, or sitting down in the masjid
making *tasbeeh'*. And we used to think that he wasn't good at
disobeying Allaah!"[171]

Stated 'Aasim al-Ahwal, *rahimahullaah*: "Fudayl Ibn 'Iyaad,
rahimahullaah, said to me: 'O you! Do not allow the people's great
number of people to busy you, for indeed the final affair will only be
about you besides them. Beware of wasting your day here and there,
for surely this is counted against you, and I have not seen anything
more beautiful in seeking or faster in catching than a new good
deed for an old bad deed."[172]

Narrated Jareer Ibn 'Abdul-Hameed, *rahimahullaah*: "An hour never
passed Sulaymaan at-Taymee except that he gave something in
charity. And if he didn't have anything to give, he would offer two
units of voluntary prayer."[173]

---

[170] *Dhayl Taareekh Baghdaad* vol. 1/pg. 354

[171] *Sifatus-Safwah* vol. 3/pg. 297

[172] *al-Hilyah* vol. 3/pg. 102

[173] *as-Siyar* vol. 6/pg. 199

Once a man said to "Umar Ibn 'Abdil-'Azeez, *rahimahullaah*: "If you would only make some free time for us?!" He responded: "Where is the free time! All the free time has gone away; there isn't any free time except with Allaah."[174]

Qataadah Ibn Khulayd, *rahimahullaah*, said: "You will never find a Believer except doing one of three things: Offering worship in the masjid, resting in a house that screens him, or handling some worldly business that is binding."[175]

Stated Yahyaa Ibn Mu'aadh, *rahimahullaah*: "The night is long so don't shorten it with your sleep and the day is pure so do not make it filthy with your sins."[176]

Moosaa Ibn Ismaa'eel, *rahimahullaah*, said: "If I said that I never once saw Hammaad Ibn Salamah laughing, I would have spoken the truth. He used to either narrate *ahaadeeth*, make *tasbeeh'*, read the Qur'aan, or offer voluntary prayer; this is how he used to split up his day."

Once Mu'aafaa Ibn 'Imraan, *rahimahullaah*, was asked: "What do you think about a man who cuts his hair or leaves it to grow long?" He answered: "It is your life, spend it however you wish!"[177]

---

[174] *Tabaqaat Ibn Sa'd* vol. 5/pg. 397

[175] *Sifatus-Safwah* vol. 3/pg. 231

[176] *Sifatus-Safwah* vol. 4/pg. 94

[177] *Sifatus-Safwah* vol. 4/pg. 180

Sufyaan, *rahimahullaah*, said: "I used to search for 'Amr Ibn Qays, *rahimahullaah*, in his shop, so if I didn't find in him in his shop I would find him in his house either offering prayer or reading the *Mushaf* as if he used to hasten towards deeds that he feared would lapse him. So if I didn't find him in his house, I would find him in the corner of one of the masjids of Koofah as if he were a thief sitting down crying. So if I didn't find him in the masjid I would find him in the graveyards sitting down crying upon himself."[178]

Hasan al-Basree, *rahimahullaah*, said: "From the signs that Allaah has turned away from the slave is that He [Allaah] preoccupies him [the slave] with that which doesn't concern him!!"[179]

---

[178] *as-Siyar* vol. 5/pg. 320

[179] *Jaami'ul-'Uloom wal-Hikam* pg. 139

Avoiding Argumentation and Debate[180]

Muslim Ibn Yasaar, *rahimahullaah*, said: "Beware of debating, for surely it is the moment of the ignorance of the scholar, and from it does the devil await his slipping."[181]

Stated ash-Shaafi'ee, *rahimahullaah*: "Debating about knowledge hardens the heart and causes mutual hatred and malice."[182]

Ibn Jurayj, *rahimahullaah*, said: "I did not extract the great knowledge from 'Ataa except with gentleness."[183]

Stated az-Zuhree, *rahimahullaah*: "Aboo Salamah, *radiyAllaahu 'anhu*, used to debate with Ibn 'Abbaas, *radiyAllaahu 'anhumma*; because of this, he was hindered from great knowledge."[184]

Maymoon Ibn Mihraan, *rahimahullaah*, said: "Do not debate with the one who is more knowledgeable than you, for if you do that he will hoard from you all his knowledge and he won't be harmed by anything that you say to him at the least."[185]

---

[180] *Min Akhbaaris-Salaf* (pg. 289-290) with abridgment

[181] *az-Zuhd* of Ahmad pg. 307

[182] *Jaami'ul-'Uloom wal-Hikam* vol. 1/pg. 519

[183] *Jaami'ul-'Uloom wal-Hikam* vol. 1/pg. 519

[184] *Jaami'ul-'Uloom wal-Hikam* vol. 1/pg. 518

[185] *Jaami'ul-'Uloom wal-Hikam* vol. 1/pg. 517

Stated Bilaal Ibn Sa'd, *rahimahullaah*: "When you see a man of great argumentation and debate, conceited with his view, then his portion of loss has become total and complete."[186]

'Abdul-Kareem al-Jazaree, *rahimahullaah*, said: "A pious man never debates."[187]

Haytham Ibn Jameel, *rahimahullaah*, was asked: "A man is well learned with regards to the affairs of the Sunnah, should he debate and argue about them? He replied, "No! However he should inform the people of the Sunnah, so if it is accepted from him then good and if not then he should keep silent."[188]

---

[186] *ash-Shu'ab* pg. 8076

[187] *as-Shu'ab* pg. 8129

[188] *Jaami'u Bayaanil-'Ilmi wa Fadlihi* vol. 4/pg. 94-quoted from the: *Fadlu 'Ilmis-Salaf* pg. 79 footnote no. 5 from the editor.

Giving Advice and Some of its Etiquettes[189]

Narrated Sufyaan, *rahimahullaah*: "Once Talhah, *rahimahullaah*, came to 'Abdul-Jabbaar Ibn Waa'il, *rahimahullaah*, while he was sitting with some people, so he whispered something to him and then left. He [Talhah] asked them: 'Do you know what he just said to me?' He said, 'Yesterday I saw that you had looked around while you were performing the prayer!'."[190]

Ibn al-Mubaarak, *rahimahullaah*, said: "Whenever a man would see something from his brother that he dislikes, he would give him orders in private and forbid him in private. Conversely, he would be rewarded for him screening his brother and also rewarded for forbidding the evil. As for today, whenever a man sees what he dislikes he angers his brother and unveils his screen."[191]

Fudayl Ibn 'Iyaad, *rahimahullaah*, said: "The Believer screens and gives sincere advice and the wicked evil doer unveils and exposes."[192]

---

189 *Min Akhbaaris-Salaf* (pg. 292)

190 *Raudatul-'Uqalaa* of Ibn Hibbaan pg. 197

191 *Raudatul-'Uqalaa* of Ibn Hibbaan pg. 197

192 *Jaami'ul-'Uloom wal-Hikam* pg. 77

Being Cautious from Giving Fatwaas[193]

Narrated 'Uqbah Ibn Muslim, *rahimahullaah*: "I accompanied Ibn
'Umar, *radiyAllaahu 'anhumaa*, for thirty-four months and very often
was he asked questions and he would say: 'I don't know'. Then he
would turn to me and say, 'Do you know what these people want
from me? They wish to make our backs a bridge for them to Hell."[194]

Ibn Mas'ood, *radiyAllaahu 'anhu*, said: "Verily, the one who gives a
fatwaa for everything the people ask him is insane."[195]

Reported Ibn Wahb, *rahimahullaah*: "Once I heard Maalik,
rahimahullaah, saying when the statement of Qaasim that reads, 'It is
better for a man to live life being ignorant than to say about Allaah
that which he doesn't know being mentioned, so he said, 'This
speech is very heavy.'"[196]

Narrated Maalik, *rahimahullaah*: "Once 'Abdullaah Ibn Naafi',
rahimahullaah, asked Ayoob as-Sakhtiyaanee, *rahimahullaah*, about
something and he didn't respond to him. He then said to him, 'I
don't think that you have understood what I asked you?' He replied,
'Of course I did' He then asked, 'So why didn't you answer me?' He
responded, 'I don't know of it.'"[197]

---

[193] *Min Akhbaaris-Salaf* (pg. 48-50) with abridgment and adjustment

[194] *Jaami'u Bayaanil-'Ilm* (vol. 2/pg. 841)

[195] *Jaami'u Bayaanil-'Ilm* (vol. 2/pg. 843)

[196] *Al-Madkhal ilas-Sunan* of al-Bayhaqee (vol. 1/pg. 435)

[197] *Jaami'u Bayaanil-'Ilm* (vol. 2/pg. 838)

Reported Ibn Wahb, *rahimahullaah*: "I heard Maalik, *rahimahullaah*, saying: "It is necessary for the scholar to become accustomed to say about what is problematic for him, *'laa adree'* [I don't know] for, surely, some good will be facilitated for him."[198]

Narrated Zayd Ibnul-Hubaab, *rahimahullaah*: "I saw Sufyaan ath-Thauree, *rahimahullaah*, saying when being asked different questions, 'I don't know' so much so that those who saw Sufyaan and didn't know who he was thought that he didn't have any knowledge."[199]

Reported Mus'ab, *rahimahullaah*: "I heard Maalik Ibn Anas, *rahimahullaah*, saying: "I have not given a *fatwaa* until seventy people attested to the reality that I was qualified for that."[200]

---

[198] *Al-Madkhal ilas-Sunan* (vol. 1/pg. 435)
[199] *Musnad Ibn al-Ja'd* (pg. 277)
[200] *Al-Hilyah* (vol. 6/pg. 316)

The Virtue of *'Ilm* [201]

Allaah, the Exalted, says: *"Allaah bears witness that laa ilaaha illa huwa (none has the right to be worshiped but He), and the angels and those having knowledge (also give this witness); (He always) maintains His creation in Justice."* *[Soorah Aali 'Imraan (3): 18]*

Ibnul-Qayyim, *rahimahullaah*, has established that this verse proves the nobility and virtue of 'ilm from three aspects:

The First: Is the fact that Allaah has used the scholars, besides the rest of the creation, to give witness which clearly proves their excellence and virtue.

The Second: Is the fact that Allaah has linked the scholars' testimony with the Oneness of Allaah and His right to be singled out in worship along with His own testimony unto Himself, the Sublime and Exalted, regarding this affair.

The Third: Entailed in Allaah calling them to witness is a praising and lauding of them because Allaah does not call any of His creation to witness except that they are pious, equitable, trustworthy, and reliable. [202]

---

[201] Source: "al-Mulim fil-Aqwaail-Mushawwiqh li Taalibil-'Ilm" (pg. 7) of Muhammad Ibn Fahd Ibn Ibraaheem al-Wad'aan with very slight abridgment

[202] *Daaru Miftaahis-Sa'aadah* (vol. 1/pg. 154)

'Alee, *radiyAllaahu 'anhu*, "*'Ilm* is better than wealth. *'Ilm* protects you
but you have to protect your wealth. Knowledge rules, but wealth is
ruled. The treasurers of wealth have died, but the treasures of *'ilm*
still remain. They are physically gone but they are present in the
people's hearts."[203]

Stated 'Abdullaah Ibn 'Abbaas, *radiyAllaahu 'anhumma*, "Reviewing
'ilm a part of the night is fonder to me than staying up the entire
night."[204]

Sufyaan ath-Thauree, *rahimahullaah*, said: "I don't know of anything
that is more virtuous than seeking Hadeeth as long as it is done
seeking Allaah's face."[205]

Stated Ibnul-Qayyim, *rahimahullaah*: "The best thing that the souls
have ever earned, the hearts have ever obtained, and the slaves
achieved therewith status in the life of this world and the next is *'ilm*
and *eemaan*. For this reason did Allaah join them together when He
said, *"And those who have been bestowed with knowledge and
faith will say: "Indeed you have stayed according to the Decree of
Allaah, until the Day of Resurrection"* [Sooratur-Room (30): 56]
He, the Exalted, also said, *"Allaah will exalt in degree those of you
who believe, and those who have been granted
knowledge."* [Sooratul-Mujaadilah (58): 11][206]

---

[203] *Adabud-Dunyaa wad-Deen* (pg. 48)]

[204] *Al-Musannaf* (vol. 11/pg. 253), *Jaami'u Bayaanil-'Ilmi wa Fadlihi* (vol.
1/pg. 117)

[205] *Tahdheeb Taareekh Dimashq* (vol. 3/pg. 345)

[206] *Al-Fawaa'id* (pg. 17)

Ibnul-Qayyim, *rahimahullaah*, also said: "If there wasn't any other virtue of *'ilm* except for nearness to the Lord of the Worlds, joining the world of the Angels, and being in the company of the highest chiefs (Angels), this would be sufficient in nobility and excellence. Then how is the case when the esteem of the life of this world and the next is attached thereto and its obtainment is its prerequisite?"[207]

Stated az-Zuhree, *rahimahullaah*: "Allaah cannot be worshiped with anything more virtuous than *'ilm.*"[208]

He, *rahimahullaah*, also said: "Allaah cannot be worshiped with something more excellent than *fiqh.*"[209]

Stated Sufyaan ath-Thauree, *rahimahullaah*: "I don't know of anything more virtuous after prophecy than spreading knowledge."[210]

He, *rahimahullaah*, also said: "There isn't any act of worship more virtuous than seeking *'ilm* as long as an individual's intention is correct."[211]

---

[207] *Daaru Miftaahis-Sa'aadah* (vol. 1/pg. 108)

[208] *Al-Bidaayah wan-Nihaayah* (vol. 9/pg. 354)

[209] *Al-Faqeeh wal-Mutafaqqih* (vol. 1/pg. 119), *Jaami'u Bayaanil-'Ilmi wa Fadlihi* (vol. 1/pg. 119)

[210] *Taareekh Baghdaad* (vol. 10/pg. 160)

[211] *Jaami'u Bayaanil-'Ilmi wa Fadlihi* (vol. 1/pg. 124)

Stated ash-Shaafi'ee, *rahimahullaah*: "Reading Hadeeth is better than voluntary prayer." He also said, "Seeking *'ilm* is more virtuous than supererogatory prayers." [212]

Qataadah Ibn Di'aamah as-Sadoosee, *rahimahullaah*, said: "A chapter of knowledge that a man memorizes, intending thereby to reform himself, his religion, and the people, is better than an entire year of worship."[213]

Stated Mutarrif Ibn 'Abdillaah, *rahimahullaah*: "The virtue of *'ilm* is better than the virtue of deeds and the best of your Religion is piety." He also said, "The virtue of *'ilm* is more beloved to me than the virtue of worship and the best of our Religion is piety."[214]

Ath-Thauree, *rahimahullaah*, used to say: "I don't know of any worship that is better than teaching the people *'ilm*." [215]

It is also said, "The similitude of the Scholars is that of water (rain), wherever it falls, the people will benefit."[216]

Stated Maalik Ibn Deenaar, *rahimahullaah*: "The people of the worldly life will leave it not having tasted the best thing therein." It

---

[212] *As- Siyar* (vol. 10/pg. 23)

[213] *Al-Bidaayah wan- Nihaayah* (vol. 9/pg. 261)

[214] *As-Siyar* (vol. 4/pg. 189)

[215] *Jaami'u Bayaanil-'Ilmi wa Fadlihi* (vol. 1/pg. 56)]

[216] *Jaami'u Bayaanil-'Ilmi wa Fadlihi* (vol. 1/pg. 56)]

was asked, 'Which is what?' He replied, "Knowledge of Allaah, the Exalted."[217]

Rabee'ah, *rahimahullaah*, said: "'*Ilm* is a means leading to every virtue."[218]

Stated Ibn Mahdee, *rahimahullaah*: "A person is in more need of '*ilm* than food and drink."[219]

Sufyaan ath-Thauree, *rahimahullaah*, said: "A person is in more need of '*ilm* than bread and meat."[220]

It is also said: "Whoever humbles himself in search of '*ilm*, he will be sought in high esteem."[221]

Stated ash-Shaafi'ee, *rahimahullaah*: "Whoever learns the Qur'aan will have great value. Whoever speaks about Fiqh, his worth will increase. Whoever writes Hadeeth, his argument will become strong. Whoever studies language, his nature will become soft. Whoever studies arithmetic his view will become abundant. Whoever does not protect himself, his '*ilm* will not benefit him."[222]

---

[217] *As-Siyar* (vol. 5/pg. 363)

[218] *As-Siyar* (vol. 6/pg. 90)

[219] *Al-Hilyah* (vol. 9/pg. 4)

[220] *Al-Hilyah* (vol. 7/pg. 659)

[221] *Zahrul-Ghusoon min Kitaabil-Funoon* (pg. 18)

[222] *As-Siyar* (vol. 10/pg. 24)

Hasan al-Basree, *rahimahullaah*, said: "For me to learn a chapter of
'ilm and teach it to a Muslim is more beloved to me than to posses
the riches of the entire worldly life and spend it in Allaah's cause."[223]

Stated Mutarrif Ibn 'Abdillaah, *rahimahullaah*: "*'Ilm* is better than
acts and deeds. See you not that the monk stands the entire night in
prayer until he wakes up and commits *shirk*!"[224]

Stated Yahyaa Ibn Abee Katheer al-Yamaamee, *rahimahullaah*:
"Teaching *fiqh* is prayer and studying the Qur'aan is prayer."[225]

Sufyaan Ibn 'Uyaynah, *rahimahullaah*, said: "The people who will
have the grandest station [in the Hereafter] are those who are
between Allaah and His creation; The Prophets and the Scholars.
Do you know the similitude of ignorance and knowledge? It is like
the land of *kufr* and the land of Islaam. For surely, if the people of
Islaam leave off *jihad*, the people of *kufr* will come and take over
Islaam. And if the people leave off knowledge they will become
ignoramuses." [226]

---

[223] *Al-Faqeeh wal-Mutafaqqih* (vol. 1/pg.102), *al-Majmoo' Sharhul-Muhadhab*
(vol. 1/pg. 21)
[224] *Al-Faqeeh wal-Mutafaqqih* (vol.1/pg.110), *Jaami'u Bayaanil-'Ilmi wa Fadlihi*
(vol. 1/pg. 116)
[225] *Al-Faqeeh wal-Mutafaqqih* (vol. 1/pg. 103)
[226] *Al-Faqeeh wal-Mutafaqqih* (vol. 1/pg. 103)]

Stated Hasaan Ibn 'Atiyyah, *rahimahullaah*: "A man never increases in *'ilm* except that he increases in closeness to the people and mercy from Allaah."[227]

---

[227] *Al-Hilyah* (vol. 6/pg. 74)

The Importance of *'Ilm* [228]

Stated Hasan al-Basree, *rahimahullaah*: "If it wasn't for the scholars,
the people would become just like animals."[229]

Ibnul-Qayyim, *rahimahullaah*, said: "The person who performs
actions without knowledge is like someone who is traveling without
a guide, and it is well known that this person is more likely to
become ruined than reach safety. Even if he happens to safely reach
his destination, then this is still blameworthy (meaning performing
deeds without knowledge), rather condemned by all of the
intellectuals. Shaykhul-Islaam Ibn Taymiyyah used to say, "Whoever
abandons the proof and evidence will be misguided and there isn't
any proof and evidence except what the Messenger, *sallAllahu 'alayhi
wa sallam*, has brought."[230]

He also said, *rahimahullaah*: "There isn't anything that is more
beloved, delicious, pleasant, and blessed to the slave's heart and life
than loving his Originator, Creator, and Lord, and constantly
making remembrance of Him, and striving hard for His good
pleasure. Moreover, this is the perfection after which there isn't any
perfection for the slave and for this reason was the creation brought
into existence. There is no path to enter that except through the
door of *'Ilm* because loving something is a branch of awareness and

---

[228] Source: "*al-Mulim fil-Aqwaalil-Mushawwiqah li-Taalibil-'Ilm*" of Dr.
Muhammad Ibn Fahd Ibn Ibraaheem al-Wad'aan (pg. 12) with very slight
abridgment and adjustment.

[229] *Mukhtasar Minhaajil-Qaasideen* (pg. 17)]

[230] *Daaru Miftaahis-Sa'aadah* (vol. 1/pg. 83)]

[66]

consciousness of it. The individuals who have the most knowledge of Allaah love Him the most. Whoever knows Allaah will love Him and whoever knows the life of this world and its people will forsake them. Thus, 'ilm opens upon this magnificent door which is the secret of the creation and the command."[231]

He also stated, rahimahullaah: "If there wasn't any other benefit of 'ilm besides the reality that it produces certainty which is the greatest means of life for the heart, and therewith exists its tranquility, strength, vigor, and the rest of the essential requirements of life, it would be sufficient in virtue. For this reason did Allaah laud its people in His Book and praise them when He, the Sublime and Exalted, said, *"And they believe with certainty the Hereafter}* *[Sooratul-Baqarah (2):4]."* And condemned those who do not have any certainty when He, the Exalted said, *"Because mankind believed not with certainty in Our aayaat [signs and proofs]"* *[Sooratun-Naml (27): 82]*[232]

Some of the Salaf used to say: "The best thing that a person can be blessed with is intellect and the worst thing that a person can be afflicted with is ignorance."[233]

Stated Aboo Muslim al-Khaulaanee, rahimahullaah: "The Scholars on earth are like the stars in the heavens. If they [the Scholars] appear for the mankind they [mankind] will be guided by them. And if they

---

[231] *Daaru Miftaahis-Sa'aadah* (vol. 1/pg. 136)]

[232] *Daaru Miftaahis-Sa'aadah* (vol. 1/pg. 136)]

[233] *Tadhkiratus-Saami' wal- Mutakallim* (pg. 25)

[the Scholars] are hidden from mankind they [mankind] will fall into disarray and confusion."

Abul-Aswad ad-Du'alee, *rahimahullaah*, said: "There isn't anything more esteemed than *'Ilm*. The kings are rulers of the people, and the Scholars are rulers of the leaders."

Stated Wahb, *rahimahullaah*: "The following things branch off from *'ilm*: Nobility even if its possessor is a person of low lineage; honor and esteem even if he is base; closeness even if he is far; wealth even if he is poor; and awe from the people even if he is inferior."[234]

❁ ❁ ❁

---

[234] *Tadhkiratus-Saami' wal- Mutakallim* (pg. 26)

Holding Fast to the Sunnah and Being Cautious of Innovations and their People[235]

'Abdullaah Ibn Mas'ood, *radiyallaahu 'anhu*, said: "Being moderate upon the Sunnah is better than working hard upon *bid'ah*."[236]

He, *radiyallaahu 'anhu*, also stated: "Follow and do not innovate for indeed, you have been sufficed; every *bid'ah* is a misguidance."[237]

Hasan al-Basree, *rahimahullaah*, stated: "No statement is correct without action, and neither a statement nor action can be correct except with an intention, and neither a statement, action or intention can be correct without the Sunnah."[238]

'Abdullaah Ibn 'Aun, *rahimahullaah*, said: "Whoever dies upon Islaam and the Sunnah will have the glad tidings of all good."[239]

Abul-'Aaliyah, *rahimahullaah*, stated: "Learn Islaam and when you have learned it, then don't abandon it. Hold fast to the straight path for indeed, it is Islaam and do not sway from the Path neither to the

---

[235] *Min Akhbaaris-Salaf* (pg. 26-35) with adbridgment and adjustment
[236] *Az-Zuhd of Ahmad* (pg. 198)
[237] *Sharh Usool 'Itiqaad Ahlis-*Sunnah (vol. 2/pg. 56)
[238] *Sharh Usool 'Itiqaad Ahlis-Sunnah* (vol. 2/pg. 56)
[239] *Sharh Usool 'Itiqaad Ahlis-Sunnah* (vol. 2/pg. 67)

right or the left, and hold fast to the Sunnah of your Prophet, *sallAllahu 'alayhi wa sallam*, and his companions."[240]

Fudayl Ibn 'Iyaad, *rahimahullaah*, said: "Follow the paths of guidance and be harmed not by the small number of those who are guided, beware of the paths of misguidance and don't be deceived by the great number of those who are in ruin."[241]

Az-Zuhree, *rahimahullaah*, stated: "Those who have past from our scholars used to say: 'Holding fast to the Sunnah is salvation'"[242]

Narrated al-Auzaa'iee, *rahimahullaah*: "It used to be said that there were five things that the companions of Muhammad, *sallAllahu 'alayhi wa sallam*, and those who followed them in goodness were upon: Sticking to the *jamaa'ah*, following the Sunnah, maintaining the masjids, reciting the Qur'aan and making *jihaad* in Allaah's cause."[243]

Reported 'Ubaydullaah Ibn Waasil, *rahimahullaah*: "I heard Ahmad as-Sirmaaree saying once after he pulled out his sword, 'Know for sure, I have killed one thousand Turks [from the disbelievers] with this sword and if it wasn't for my fear of it being an act of innovation I would order for it to be buried with me!'"[244]

---

[240] Al-Hilyah (vol. 2/pg. 218)

[241] Al-'Itisaam (pg. 62)

[242] Al-Hilyah (vol. 3/pg. 369)

[243] Al-Hilyah (vol. 8/pg. 142)

[244] As-Siyar (vol. 13/pg. 39)

Sufyaan ath-Thauree, *rahimahullaah*, said: "Treat the People of the
Sunnah kindly, for indeed, they are strangers." He also said: "If one
man is in the east and another in the west, and they are both from
the people of the Sunnah, then send them the salaams and make
du'aa for them; how few are the people of Ahlus-Sunnah wal-
Jamaa'ah."[245]

Narrated 'Abdur-Rahmaan Ibn Abiz-Zinaad, *rahimahullaah*, from his
father who said: "I have never seen anyone more knowledgeable of
the Sunnah then Qaasim Ibn Muhammad, and a man was not
considered a real man until he knew the Sunnah."[246]

Ayoob as-Sakhtiyaanee, *rahimahullaah*, said: "Indeed, the death of a
man from the Ahlus-Sunnah reaches me and I feel as if I have lost
one of my limbs."[247]

Once Sa'eed Ibn al-Musayyib, *rahimahullaah*, saw a man making a lot
of rukoo' and sujood after fajr so he forbade him. The man replied
back to him, 'O Aboo Muhammad! Will Allaah punish me for
making salaat?' He replied, 'No, but however He will punish you for
opposing the Sunnah."[248]

---

[245] *Sharh Usool 'Itiqaad Ahlis-Sunnah* (vol. 2/pg. 64)

[246] *Al-Hilyah* (vol. 2/pg. 184)

[247] *Al-Hilyah* (vol. 3/pg 9)

[248] *At-Tamheed* (vol. 20/pg. 104)

Whenever a man makes an innovation, the sweetness of hadeeth is removed from his heart."[249]

Reported Ismaa'eel Ibn Naafi, *rahimahullaah*: 'Abdullaah Ibn al-Mubaarak, *rahimahullaah*, said: "Know for sure o my brother, nowadays death is an honorable thing for every Muslim who meets Allaah upon the Sunnah, and indeed unto Allaah we belong and unto Him we shall surely return. Certainly, we complain to Allaah, about the lack of helpers, prevalence of innovations and unto Allah do we complain about the calamities that have befallen this nation such as the going away of the scholars and Ahlus-Sunnah and the prevalence of innovations."[250]

Once Aboo Zur'ah, *rahimahullaah*, was asked about the books of Haarith al-Muhaasabee and said: "Beware of these books, these books are books of innovations and acts of misguidance. Hold fast to the *athar* and you will certainty find sufficiency from that which is in these books." He was then asked, 'In these books is a lesson?' He answered: "Whoever does not find a lesson in the Book of Allaah, then he won't ever find a lesson in these books."[251]

Stated Ibn al-Mubaarak, *rahimahullaah*: "Beware of sitting with a person of innovations."[252]

---

[249] *As-Siyar* (vol. 12/pg. 245)

[250] *Al-Bida' of Ibn* Waddaah (pg. 97)

[251] *Taareekh Baghdaad* (vol. 8/pg. 215)

[252] *As-Siyar* (vol. 8/pg. 411)

Narrated 'Aasim al-Ahwal, *rahimahullaah*: "Once I sat with
Qataadah, *rahimahullaah*, and 'Amr Ibn 'Ubayd, *rahimahullaah*, was
mentioned, so he began to speak ill about him and take stabs at
him. So I cried out, 'O Aboo al-Khattaab! I should not find the
scholars speaking ill and taking stabs at each other.' He responded:
'O you small cross-eyed one! Don't you realize that whenever a man
commits innovations, then they should be mentioned in order that
they are avoided.'"[253]

Matr al-Warraaq, *rahimahullaah*, said: "A few deeds from the Sunnah
is better than many deeds of bid'ah. Whoever performs a deed from
the Sunnah Allah will accept it from him. And whoever performs an
act of bid'ah Allah will reject his bid'ah."[254]

Reported Sa'eed Ibn 'Aamir, *rahimahullaah*: "Sulaymaan at-Taymee,
rahimahullaah, became extremely ill and began to cry greatly. So he
was asked, 'What causes you to cry? Are you in unrest from death?'
He responded, 'No, but however once I passed by a *qadaree* and gave
him the salaams, so I fear that my Lord, the Mighty and Majestic,
will take me to account for that!'"[255]

Aboo Qilaabah, *rahimahullaah*, said: "Do not sit with the people of
desires, nor debate with them, for indeed, I don't feel safe that they
won't drench you in their misguidance and confuse you with regards
to that which you used to know."[256]

---

[253] Al-Hilyah (vol. 2/pg. 335)
[254] Al-HIlyah (vol. 3/pg. 76)
[255] Al-Hilyah (vol. 3/pg. 32)
[256] Ash-Shu'ab (vol. 7.pg. 60)

Stated Hasan al-Basree, *rahimahullaah*: "Do not sit with a person of innovations, for surely he will disease your heart."[257]

Reported Hasan Ibn Shaqeeq, *rahimahullaah*: "Once we were with Ibn al-Mubaarak, *rahimahullaah*, when a man came to him, so he asked him, 'Are you that *jahmee*?' The man replied, 'Yes'. He then said to the man, 'When you leave me then don't come back to me.' The man then said, 'I have repented.' He said to him, 'No, until your repentance becomes clear the likes of which was clear from your innovation.'"[258]

Sa'eed Ibn Jubayr, *rahimahullaah*, said: "For my son to accompany a wicked sinner is more beloved to me than for him to accompany an innovator who performs great worship."[259]

---

[257] *Al-'Itisaam* (pg. 62)
[258] *Ash-Sharh wal-Ibaanah* (pg. 166)
[259] *Ash-Sharh wal-Ibaanah* (pg. 149)

Virtues, Etiquettes and Rulings of Fasting According to the Pure Sunnah[260]

The First Hadeeth

The Incumbency of Fasting and some of its Wisdoms

One the authority of 'Abdullaah Ibn 'Umar, *radiyallaahu 'anhumaa*, who reported that the Prophet, *sallAllahu 'alayhi wa sallam*, said: **"Islaam is built upon five things: The testimony that there is no deity worthy of worship besides Allaah, and Muhammad is the Messenger of Allaah, establishing the prayer, paying zakaat, offering the pilgrimage to the Sacred House and fasting Ramadaan."[261]**

In this hadeeth is a proof citing the incumbency of fasting Ramadaan and the fact that it is from the pillars of Islam and its major foundations which Allaah, the Exalted, has made obligatory upon His slaves for many magnificent wisdoms and brilliant secrets; whoever realizes them realizes them and whoever is ignorant of them is ignorant of them.

---

[260] *"Mukhtasar Ahaadeeth as-Siyaam Ahkaam wa Aadaab"* of 'Abdullaah Ibn Saalih al-Fauzaan (pg. 7-9)

[261] Collected by al-Bukhaaree (no. 8) and Muslim (no. 16)

From the Wisdoms of Fasting and its Secrets are:

1- It is an act of worship to Allaah, the Exalted, with which the slave seeks nearness to his Lord by leaving off what he is fond of and desires, by obeying his Lord, and complying with His commands. So by this, the truth of his faith, perfection of his worship, strength of his love, and hope of Allaah's reward manifests. This is because he [the slave] knows that the good pleasure of his Lord is entailed in leaving off his lusts, so he puts forth His good pleasure before his own desires.

2- For this reason, there are many Believers who would prefer to be beaten or imprisoned rather than to break their fast one day in Ramadaan without a valid excuse.

3- It is a reason behind obtaining at-Taqwaa and purification of the soul by obeying Allaah in that which He has commanded and avoiding that which He has forbidden. He, the Exalted, says: *"O you who believe! Observing fasting is prescribed for you as it was prescribed for those before you that you have at- Taqwaa." [Soorah al-Baqarah 2: (183)]* At-Taqwaa comprehensively includes all good of this life and the Hereafter and hence all fruits of fasting stem forth from it.

4- Holding one's soul back from lusts, weaning it from things that it is accustomed to and narrowing the paths of the devil towards the slave by constricting food and drink. Hence, Shaytaan's penetration into the slave becomes weak, and conversely, acts of disobedience from him [the slave] are drastically lessened.

[76]

5- The heart becomes pure, undisturbed and void which allows it to think correctly, reflect and make remembrance of Allaah. This is because the intake of lusts and desires hardens the heart and blinds it from realizing the truth. As for fasting, then it safeguards the strength and health of both the heart and the bodily limbs.

6- Coming to know of Allaah's bounties and favors upon the slave by blessing him to be able to become full and quench his thirst throughout the entire year. When he fasts he reflects on the hunger pains of the poor, needy people. Thus, he thanks his Lord and feels the pains of his poor brethren; and the favors and bounties of Allaah cannot be truly appreciated until they go away.

7- Many health benefits are obtained by lessening the amount of food, protecting the health by properly arranging meal times and reviving the digestive system for specific periods of time. In short, the wisdoms of fasting are magnificent and its benefits are countless. Allaah has made as a result of it endless rewards and tremendous incentives of such grand multitude that if the fasting soul were to imagine them, it would take flight into the sky out of happiness in hoping that the entire year would be Ramadaan.

O Allaah! Grant us the success to follow the guidance, keep us away from the reasons of destruction and misery, bless us with understanding in the religion and dying upon the Sunnah of the last of the Prophets, and forgive us, our parents [who are Muslims] and all of the Muslims.

❀ ❀ ❀

Questions and Answers by Shaykh Hasan Ibn 'Abdul-Wahhaab al-Bannah, may Allaah preserve him[262]

Q. 1: What is the ruling with regards to the one who does not offer the obligatory prayers yet he offers the *Jumu'ah* prayer?

A. 1: "Anyone who offers *Salaatul Jumu'ah* is doing a lot of good; however he is missing a lot of blessings by not offering the obligatory prayers. It is best to do both, meaning offer the obligatory prayers and *Salaatul Jumu'ah*. During the prayer, it is upon the Muslim to be in the state of purity. He should be sincere in prayer and when making *du'aa*, which should all be done for the sake of Allaah. This is what causes the heart to become tranquil. So why is it that this individual doesn't offer prayer? The prayer prohibits all wrong doing, and Allaah remembers you when you remember Him. So why is it that you don't want to offer prayer?

Q. 2: On *Yaumul Jumu'ah* while we are waiting for the Imam to begin delivering his *khutbah*, which is roughly about forty-five minutes, some of the brothers are playing around, being loud and disruptive. We have asked them several times to read the Qur'aan and *ahaadeeth* of the Prophet, may the peace and blessing of Allaah be upon him, however they are still loud and disruptive. Therefore, we have decided to give a short advice or reminder

---

[262] All of the following questions and answers were presented to and answered by the noble Shaykh, may Allaah give him well being, during his visit to the Muslims at Northern State Prison located in Newark, New Jersey on Monday, July 21, 2008.

[78]

until the Imam arrives. Is this permissible and if not what do you advise us to do in this particular situation?

A. 2: "Yes, this is permissible according to your circumstances. Umar Ibn al-Khattaab [perhaps this should read: 'Uthmaan Ibn 'Afaan, may Allaah be pleased with them both] ordered two *adhaans* to be called for *Salaatul-Jumu'ah*, while there was only one *adhaan* during the time of the Messenger of Allaah, may the peace and blessings of Allaah be upon him, was alive. The first *adhaan* was to remind the people who were in the marketplaces that *Salaatul Jumu'ah* was about to begin and the second *adhaan* was to signal the start of *Salaatul Jumu'ah*."

Q. 3: "Here in our current environment we are without a masjid, however the gymnasium is the place where we have *Salaatul Jumu'ah*. Some of the brothers take the position that since we gather in the gymnasium for *Salaatul Jumu'ah* it is permissible to pray two *rak'ah* even though the gym is not considered a masjid. Is this correct?

A. 3: "This is permissible to do this in the masjid or in any place as long as you have a place where you call the *adhaan* for prayer."

Q. 4: It has been narrated that the Messenger of Allaah, may the peace and blessings of Allaah be upon him, said: "*The prayer is not accepted for forty days from the one who consumes intoxicants.*" Oh noble Shaykh, if one continues to drink alcoholic beverages does the total amount of days that Allaah doesn't accept his prayers continue to increase from forty days to eighty days, etc...?

[79]

A. 4: "What is important here is that if a Muslim is intoxicated, then it is not permissible for him to offer prayer until he is sober. The drinking of alcoholic beverages is a sin, however it is not *shirk*. If a person engages in drinking alcohol, then he should ask Allaah to forgive him."

Q. 5: We have brothers here who indulge heavily in the drinking of alcoholic beverages and therefore put their brothers in harm's way by way of these evil deeds. After we advise them about the dangers of drinking alcohol, they continue to engage in this sinful act. Is it permissible to boycott these brothers for this reason?

A 5: "If someone is steadily increasing in committing sins and we decide that they should be boycotted, the evil ones from the *shayaateen* (devils) will take them and cause them to join them. Therefore, boycotting them will make the matter more severe. It is best to keep advising them and do not let the *shayaateen* (devils) take them, which will hurt the Muslim body as a whole. This is an important learning process for us all."

Q. 6: I have noticed that there are several *fataawaa* mentioning the fact that raising the hands immediately after prayer is not correct. Do they mean raising the hands immediately after the prayer without making *dhikr* and *tasbeeh'* or are they referring to the impermissibility of not raising them at all?

A. 6: "It is permissible to raise your hands while making *du'aa* at any time when you are not praying. However, it is permissible to raise your hands while offering the *Salaatul Witr*."

[80]

Q. 7: "Is it permissible to have dreadlocks? (One of the brothers in attendance at the lecture stood up in order for the Shaykh to see his dreadlocks)?

A. 7: "This is not permissible. The Prophet, may the peace and blessing be upon him, sometimes used to have braids, but not like these. [Look further into this]

Q. 8: There are Muslims who join the "Bloods" (The name of a particular gang) wherein they make a *bai'ah* (pledge) of allegiance to them. Is this permissible?

A. 8: "This type of *bai'ah* is not permissible and is a *bid'ah* (innovation). The *bai'ah* can only be given to an *amir* or *haakim* [a Muslim leader or governor of a country or region]. A side note: There was a companion who drank the blood of the Messenger of Allaah, may the peace and blessings of Allaah be upon him,, however this was exclusively for him and not for Abu Bakr, 'Umar, 'Uthmaan or 'Ali, may Allaah be pleased with them all. (Shaykh Hasan was unclear as to whether or not the Muslim who joined the "Bloods" had to drink blood, therefore prompting him to mention this side note).

Q. 9: Is it permissible to offer the prayer with those Muslims who are "Bloods" (The name of a particular gang) even though we do not feel safe around them? They continue to have affiliations with the "Bloods" and also commit unlawful acts with them.

A. 9: "You should always be careful of the ignorance of a non-Muslim or a sinful Muslim. Each and every one of you present here is responsible for what he knows. If one of you doesn't know about a particular matter, then you have an excuse. However, if you do know, then you are responsible for your actions. For the one who doesn't know, then it is best to continue advising him and keep him close to the Muslims. Then, if he continues to engage in the *haraam* acts, then you have a right to keep away from him due to the fact that we don't want to be affected by his evil. If this is the case, then continue to give him advice, but from a distance."

Q. 10: What are the best books to read in the affairs of '*aqeedah*?

A. 10: The best books in the affairs of '*aqeedah* are those books from the known scholars of the Sunnah. These books are:

- *Al-Usool at-Thalaathah*
- *Al-Usool as-Sittah*
- *Kashuf-Shubuhaat*
- *Al-Qawaa'id al-Arba'ah*
- *Nawaaqidul-Islaam*
- *Fathul-Majeed*
- *Al-'Aqeedah al-Waasitiyyah*
- *Tafseer As-Sa'adee*

There are certain beginning levels that the seeker of knowledge must go through in order to progress to higher levels. These books are for those who are beginning the journey towards seeking knowledge. You should have knowledge of these books even if it means taking fifteen minutes per day in order to read and understand them. For example, it is possible for you to organize your time in a way that allows you to take a few minutes after each of the five daily prayers and read one of the books previously mentioned. This can be done alone or if possible together with your Muslim brothers."

Questions and Answers with Shaykh Hasan Ibn 'Abdul-Wahhaab from his Visit to Chicago, IL

Q. 1: What is the minimum number of people that must be present in order to establish *jumu'ah*? Is it 1, 2, or 3?

A. 1: Three people are needed in order to establish *Salaatul Jumu'ah*.

Q. 2: Is it waajib (obligatory) for a Muslim who is incarcerated to attend *Salaatul Jumu'ah*?

A. 2: Yes, if *Salaatul Jumu'ah* is offered then it is waajib for him to attend *Salaatul Jumu'ah*.

Q. 3: In the prison that I'm currently at, there are some Muslims .who claim *Salafiyyah* but don't attend *Salaatul Jumu'ah* until after the *khutbah* is over with the intention of only praying the *salaat*. The reason 'for them not attending the *khutbah* is due to the imam not being salafee. Is this permissible?

A. 3: No, this is not permissible. They should attend the *khutbah* because it is important. In it contains a lot of good. If the *khutbah* contains both *sunnah* and bid'ah, then accept that which is from the *sunnah* and reject that which contains bid'ah. Don't cause division between the Muslims within the prison.

Q. 4: Do sinful acts like listening to music, playing chess, and playing cards remove one from *Salafiyyah* especially after he has been given advice about the dangers of these matters?

[84]

A. 4: The likes of these acts are indeed sins, however if this person is
salafee in his statements, his actions, as well as in his heart, then
these sins does not remove him from *Salafiyyah*. It is upon anyone
who commits sins that they ask Allah for forgiveness. Everyone
commits sins and you will never find anyone who never commits
sins.

Q. 5: We have a brother who prays with us, however when he
prays with us his physical condition causes him to sit down in a
wheelchair or chair while we are praying. How should the brother
line up with us when praying?

A. 5: Anyone who prays in congregation while sitting should align
his shoulders with the other brother's shoulders and if possible he
should pray at the end of the row.

Q. 6: Before one makes *wudoo,* is it waajib for him to say
"*a'oodhu billaahi min Shaytaanir Rajeem min hamzihi wa
nafkhihi?*

A. 6: One should say this particular du'aa for the salaat and not
wudoo. Prior to making *wudoo,* one should recite "*a'oodhu billaahi min
Shaytaanir Rajeem.*"

Q. 7: Yaa Shaykh, what is your advice to the Muslim who doesn't
pray. We have advised him on numerous occasions along with
providing numerous proofs and evidences to him. We are aware
about the importance of advising one another for the sake of
Allaah and also being patient. However, his leaving off the prayer
has left him to the disposal of the *Shaytaan* and now he's starting

to cause fitnah between us Muslims and the non-Muslims within
the prison?

A. 7: You should make *du'aa* for him and continue to be gentle with
him and also make sure you speak to him with kind words. Don't
argue with him and always advise him with politeness. It is upon
you to be patient with him.

Q. 8: I'm a Muslim sister who is incarcerated with no other
Muslim sisters around me. Is there any advice that you can
provide me with?

A. 8: I advise you with patience and to read the Qur'aan and to pray
both the obligatory prayers as well as the *sunnah* prayers. You should
also fast and always remember Allaah in everything you do.

Q. 9: Is it possible for you to provide us with some narrations of
some of the scholars from the past such as Shaykhul-Islaam Ibn
Taymiyyah and Imam Ahmad Ibn Hanbal, *rahimahullaah*, who
were imprisoned and how they dealt with the hardships of being
imprisoned?

A. 9: What comes to mind right now is the statement of Shaykhul-
Islaam Ibn Taymiyyah when he said, "Paradise is in my heart, so
how can they do this to me"!

Q. 10: What advice can you provide regarding how should one
spend his time while imprisoned?

A. 10: One should read the Qur'aan and Islamic books. He should

also make sure that he prays his obligatory prayers. He should also
find a job such as carpentry in order to work.

Q. 11: Which books should we read?

A. 11: You should read *tafseer* of the Qur'aan and the various
explanations of *Saheeh al-Bukhaaree* and *Muslim*. You should also
read other books on Islamic history such as "*al Bidaayah wan-
Nihaayah*" (The Beginning to the End) by Shaykhul-Islaam Ibn
Katheer. I also encourage you to read about the history before the
time of the Messenger of Allaah, may the peace and blessings of
Allaah be upon him.

Questions and Answers with Shaykh Hasan Ibn 'Abdul-Wahhaab and the Shooraa of Masjid al-Ihsaan From His Visit to Flint, MI

Q. 1. The prison administration hired someone from amongst the Muslims as the Islamic chaplain and he opposes *Salafiyyah* in general. Am I correct in my understanding that he is merely a liaison for the Muslims in that prison to the administration and not an *imaam* over the Muslims? Am I required to call him "*Imaam*"?

A. 1: What is important here is that this individual should be concerned with establishing the *salaat* with the *jamaa'ah* (general body of the Muslims). It is from the *manhaj* of *Ahlus-Sunnah wal-Jamaa'ah* that one prays behind every Muslim, even if he was a person known for his evil. This individual should strive to use wisdom by making attempts to call him to the way of the *Salaf*. It is the prison administration's decision to choose the *imaam* at that facility. Therefore, there is really nothing that you can do regarding this issue and if you tried to do something to change the situation, then this could cause harm to you. The best thing for you to do is to advise with good character and make *du'aa* for him in hope that he changes his position.

Q. 2: What is the ruling on greeting and hugging another Muslim everyday and every time you see him. Is there a time period that should be elapsed between seeing one another wherein it justifies such an embrace? This seems to have become commonplace when certain groups meet.

[88]

A. 2: Greeting and shaking hands with one another for the sake of
Allaah is something that is good and it removes sins. However, to
do it every time is not recommended. However, as for hugging every
time that you see one another, then this is not from the *Sunnah*.
What is from the *Sunnah* is hugging or embracing one who has been
traveling or has been away for some time. This is a good time to
greet and hug your Muslim brother.

**Q. 3: Many Muslims, more and more each day are taking
medically prescribed psychotropic drugs due to them not being
able to cope wit being imprisoned. They say these drugs help them
sleep away the horrors of their miserable state. However, there are
others who take these drugs in order to silence the voices that they
claim to hear in their heads. What advice do you have for these
brothers?**

A. 3: The Muslims who use these medically prescribed psychotropic
drugs due to them not being able to cope with being imprisoned,
this medication has the same effect as an intoxicant, which is
haraam (impermissible). One should not engage in these types of
acts, but rather they should take advantage of their time by reading
the Qur'aan and the many books of the *Sunnah*, making *salaat*,
fasting, and enjoying the company of their Muslim brothers. They
should also make attempts to communicate with their family and
loved ones. They should also make *du'aa* to Allaah and ask for His
forgiveness. For example, the Prophet Yusuf (Joseph), may Allaah's
peace and blessings be upon him, was in prison for several years and
he was patient with Allaah's decree. Therefore, it is upon the
Muslims to exercise patience while in prison. Just because the
Prophet Yusuf, may Allaah's peace and blessings be upon him, was a

very noble and strong willed man and some of you Muslims are in a weakened state doesn't justify using these types of medications due to not being able to cope. It is better for the imprisoned Muslims to focus on worshipping their Lord and learning their deen as opposed to being free and putting themselves in harm's way of committing sinful acts such as drinking, gambling, using illegal drugs, partying and being with women. Another example is Shaykhul-Islam Ibn Taymiyyah, may Allaah have mercy on him. While he was in prison, he used to spend his time studying the religion and sometimes when the prison guards took away his pen and paper, he would use chalk in order to write an *ayah* from the Qur'aan or write *ahaadeeth* that he memorized on the prison wall.

Fataawaa From the Mashaayikh and 'Ulamaa

Q. 1: "Here at W.C.I, we are surrounded by mountains on all sides. We have prayer calendars but we still notice that the calender may say that *salaatul Fajr* comes in at 6:00 am or today at 4:50 am but yet we don't see the first light until about 5:20 am for example. As well as salaatul Maghrib, the calendar may say that it comes in at 8:20 pm but the sun goes past the mountains at about 7:50 pm. So our question is: Should we go by the calendar or the signs of the sun and how it comes over the mountains and how it goes under the mountains?

A. 1: Shaykh 'Abdullaah Ibn 'Ateeq al-Mutarrafee, may Allaah preserve him, said: "No, instead they should go by the schedule or prayer calendar because by them being surrounded by mountains, they may think that the sun has set, but in reality it hasn't' set and it can still be seen by those who are not surrounded by those mountains..."

Q. 2: Some people are under the understanding that you should raise your hands only four times in the prayer using the hadeeth of Ibn 'Umar who he said: The Prophet, *sallAllahu 'alayhi wa sallam,* used to raise his hands when he made *takbeer* for the prayer, when he went to *rukoo',* when he came out of *rukoo'* and at the start of the third *rak'ah.* Others as myself understand it as raising the hands at the opening takbeer, at every *rukoo',* and coming from *rukoo',* not just in the first *rak'ah,* and at the beginning of the third *rak'ah.* So my question is: Should we raise the hands only four times in the entire prayer (not including *salaatul Fajr*), only raising them at the first *rukoo'* and coming from the *rukoo',*

[91]

or should the hands be raised at every *rukoo'* and coming from *rukoo*? (Making the number 10 in a prayer of 4 *raka'aat*)?

A. 2: Shaykh 'Abdullaah Ibn 'Ateeq al-Mutarrafee, may Allaah preserve him, responded by saying: "No, this is an incorrect understanding; rather the desired meaning is in each *rak'ah*. And how can a person know what he is to do in the rest of the *raka'aat* except by the first *rak'ah*, so the number is not resticted."

Q. 3: Sometimes we are forced to cell-up with homosexuals. Should we stay in the cell with them and be patient until we can move or should we refuse to go in the cell and consequently be put in the hole for 30 days? There is only these two options so what should we do?

A. 3: Shaykh Saalih' Ibn 'Abdil-'Azeez as-Sindee, may Allaah give him the success, said: "Firstly: Refuge is sought with Allaah. Secondly: You are required to be patient in this situation, and realize that the Companions, may Allaah be pleased with them, went through things that were much worse than this and they practiced patience and perserverance. You are incarcerrated, what can you do? You don't control your own affairs, there isn't much in your hands in the likes of these situations, I mean being in prison. Thirdly: If a person feels that being put in "the hole" for thirty days by himself in the dark won't effect him mentally or in his religion, whereas maybe he can review the Qur'aan in this time period and this is better for him than being forced to cell-up with this digusting homosexual then this is one case. As for if he fears that this stay in "the hole" will affect him mentally or affect his deen, by causing him serious depression, mental problems, and the likes; then he should be patient and stay in the cell with the homosexual. He should try to avoid him as much as possible, and also try not to come in contact with him when he is undressed, and staying in the cell with him in the times in which he doesn't have to. Fourthly and lastly: You must know that there is no legislative prohibition of staying in the cell with this homosexual in this tight situation that you are in, meaning in prison. There isn't any sin upon you because you are being forced to cell up with him, *na'am*."

Q. 4: How do we line up for prayer with those brothers who use chairs to pray in because they cannot stand? Do we line up with them by their heels, or by their shoulders being lined up with our shoulders?

A. 4: Shaykh 'Abdullaah al-Bukhaaree, may Allaah preserve him, replied: "This affair is simple and there is no difficulty therein whatsoever. They should line up with your bodies, meaning their shoulders should be aligned with your shoulders."

Q. 5: In our prison we are allowed to establish *salaatul Jumu'ah* every week, *wal Hamdullillaah*. However, the *khateeb* speaks ill of *Ahlus-Sunnah*, curses, defiles and defames them in the *khutbah*, along with spitting malicious and poisonous doubts regarding the *Sunnah* and *Salafiyyah*. Some of the brothers have began to intentionally attend the *Jumu'ah* late so that they won't have to hear his *khutbah* and if they come at the end and he is still speaking they stick their fingers in their ears so that they won't hear his evil speech. So what should we do in this situation and what is most appropriate?

[93]

A. 5: Shaykh Muhammad Ibn Haadee, may Allaah preserve him,
responded by saying: "The likes of this evil man should not be
prayed behind, he should not be prayed behind at all. As long as he
curses the *Salafees* and defiles the people of the *Sunnah*, they should
not pray behind him, and did you mention that he spreads
shubuhaat [doubts and ambiguities] in his *khutbah*? [The questioner
says: Yes] Then they must pray behind someone else who does not
do so. As for them being in prison and this is the only *Jumu'ah*
prayer that is established therein, then they are required to go to
administration and those in charge of this facility and complain
about this man until he is removed and replaced with someone else,
na'am."

**Q. 6: Is it permissible for the incarcerated Muslims to pray and
celebrate the *'eid* along with different groups of the disbelievers
and polytheists who are incarcerated along with us here in the
prison?**

A. 6: Shaykh Saalih as-Sindee, may Allaah preserve him, said: "As
for praying the *'eid* prayer meaning joining religions and saying that
the Jews, Christians, and other groups of polytheists and atheists are
are our brothers in the religion, then this is a complete disaster and
castrophe. As for if you mean that some of the disbelievers may
come to the prayer or the *khutbah* for *'eid*, or express their happiness
along with the Muslims on the day of *'eid*, so one the Muslims says:
"I'm not going to be happy because these *kuffar* are happy.", or "I
won't offer the *'eid* prayer because this *kaafir* came.", and the likes of
this, then no. You Muslims should pray the *'eid* and show happiness
and the other legislated things of celebration that are from the
Sunnah and don't worry about what the disbelievers are doing. Once

again, as for the ideology that some of the Muslims may have in the prison whether they are part of administration of inmates, that the Jews and Christians are our brothers and they they aren't disbelievers, etc... This is incorrect and totally false. So therefore, you must make a difference between the two different situations or scenarios."

Q. 7: When we say *aameen* in the prayer behind the *imaam*, should we elongate or not?

A. 7: Shaykh 'Ubayd al-Jaabireee, may Allaah preserve him, said: "*Na'am, aameen* should be elongated."

Q. 8: When a person comes late to the congregational prayer and he finds that there is room in the row in front of another person, am I allowed to push him forward because I have learned that it is not from the *Sunnah* to pull him back so that I can pray with him and not be the only person in the last row?

A. 8: Shaykh Muhammad Ibn Haadee al-Madkhalee, may Allaah preserve him, answered: "You are allowed to enter into the row and try to make space if you see an opening to the best of your ability without disturbing those offering the prayer in the row ahead of you. You are also allowed to wait if it seems likely that someone else will come and then you line up with him in the row. If you don't find anyone else, then you are allowed to stand on the right side of the *imaam* in this situation as long as you don't push through the row and disturb the others praying. If there is no room on the right side of the *imaam* and no one comes, then you are excused and allowed to offer the prayer by yourself."

[95]

Q. 9: What is the explanation of the hadeeth stating that Allaah will put a seal on the heart of the one who misses three *jumu'ahs* consecutively? And does this mean that if a brother who misses three or more *jumu'ahs* without a valid excuse gives you the *salaams* then you shouldn't return the greetings to him?

A. 9: Shaykh 'Abdul-Mushin al-'Abbaad al-Badr, may Allaah preserve him, said: "The *salaams* should be returned to him and advice should be given to him, he should not be cut off without being given *naseehah*."

Shaykh Tarheeb ad-Dausiree, may Allaah preserve him, said: "Upon all circumstances, this man should be advised, you should make him be afraid of Allaah by mentioning the texts that bring fear to the heart, to him. This does not mean that he is a disbeliever; instead the only reason why he left those *jumu'ahs* off is because of weak *eemaan*. It is feared that if you boycott him, then he will become worse and become more far away from Allaah. He must be advised and have these affairs clarified to him."

Q. 10: Some brothers say that because we hold *jumu'ah* in the institution's visiting room; that it's not actually *jumu'ah* and it does not fall under the obligation to attend it. Could you please clarify this matter?

A. 10: Shaykh 'Abdul-Muhsin al-'Abbaad al-Badr, may Allaah preserve him, said: "No, this is incorrect. The Muslims who are incarcerated in this facility are required to attend this *jumu'ah*."

[96]

**Q. 11: Is the Muslim who is incarcerated required to pay the
Zakaat of his wealth if it reaches the obligatory amount and is
stored away for an entire year, and he has the ability to pay it
whereas it is kept with one of his family members or friends
outside of the prison or in a bank account?**

A. 11: Shaykh Wasiyallaah al-'Abbaas, may Allaah preserve him,
said: "Yes, as long as it reaches the obligatory amount, an entire year
passes over it, and it is easy for someone to pay it for him outside of
the prison. If they have the ability to pay the *Zakaat* for him, then it
must be paid; as for if his wealth is in a bank account and the bank
refuses to allow withdrawal from anyone besides the account holder,
then this is a different ruling. But when he leaves the prison and
comes home, then he is required to pay *Zakaat* on his wealth that
was stored when he was incarcerated, *na'am*."

**Q. 12: How does the incarcerated Muslim go about living his daily
life in the prison despite the different things that he is put
through which opposes the *Sharee'ah* such as strip searches and
being forced to offer the prayer in places that are prohibited?**

A. 12: Shaykh Saalih az-Zubaydee, may Allaah preserve him, said:
"This question can be answered from two different angles: The first:
If the Muslim was incarcerated because of a crime that he did, then
he should consider this as a purification and expiation for his sinful
crime. The second: If the Muslim was wrongly incarcerated and he
is oppressed, then he must be patient and content seeking the
reward from his Lord, the Exalted, therefore the entire affair of the
Believer is good for him. As for that which pertains to the
difficulties, hardships, trials and tribulations that he may face while

[97]

incarcerated, then he must look into the affairs. He is in a very
difficult situation over which he doesn't' have much control, so he
must be patient and level headed during all times. The shaykh
asked: "What maybe the consequence if he refuses to allow them to
strip search him?" The questioner replies: "Perhaps he will be
punished by being put in a dark isolated room by himself for a long
period of time, maybe an entire month; they call this place the
'hole'". The shaykh went on to say: "If he has the ability to be
patient being put in "the hole," and this won't affect him then
maybe this is better. This is one way of looking at this situation.
Another way of looking at it is: If he is put in "the hole" then how
can he offer the correct purification, *wudoo'*, *ghusl*, *istinjaa'*,
tayammum and so and so forth? How can he offer the prayer with his
Muslim brothers in congregation? What about *jumu'ah*? So maybe it
will be a bigger harm in him being put in "the hole" and he will be
deprived of much good and prevented from many acts of worship
that are incumbent upon him. Also, if he allows the guards to
search him once, the next time they might believe him and hold
him to be honest and he won't be forced to be violated over again.
But if he refuses, then perhaps things will be difficult for him each
time and they might say, "You Muslims don't follow the rules, so we
have to be strict on you;" and the like of this harshness. Therefore,
it is upon the incarcerated Muslims to look at what harm is greater
and take the lesser of the two." The questioner interjected and
asked: "O shaykh, it is as if you are saying that the brothers must
take the major rule of *fiqh* that reads: "When it is binding for one of
two harmful things to happen, then you bear the lesser of the two"
into play, in many instances and constantly keep this rule in their
minds in the prison?" The shaykh says: "Yes, of course, exactly right;
this is extremely important. Look at the bigger harm if it is a must

that you go through some harm. As for the part of your question about offering the prayer in places that may be filthy and the likes, then the origin of this what Allaah says in the Qur'aan: *"Fear Allaah to best of your ability."* *[Soorah At-Taghabun (64):16]* So if you, the Muslim, has the ability to offer *wudoo*, then he must offer *wudoo*. If not, then he must perform *tayammum*. If he is in a state of ritual impurity and needs to perform *ghusl*, then he performs *ghusl*; if not then *tayammum*, and etc... As for offering the prayer in a place that is prohibited such as the bathroom or on a filthy surface or, as you have mentioned in the question that the toilet is in the same room that they sleep in, then fear Allaah to best of your ability, offer the prayer standing up if you can, if not then sitting down, if not then lying down and so on so forth. As for if he is forced to pray over a toilet or a filthy surface and he doesn't have any mat or rug to cover the filth, then he should not make sujood upon filth or upon a toilet. Instead he just makes a signal with his head and so and so forth."

Q. 13: Is a Muslim man allowed to wear his head in braids, locks, and the likes, and when he offers the prayer should he take them out so that his hair can prostate along with him?

A. 13: Shaykh Tarheeb ad-Dausiree, may Allaah preserve him, answered by saying: "It is best that he stay far away from wearing his head in braids, locks, and the likes. As for when he offers the prayer and *sujood*, then it is best that he take them out so that his hair can prostrate along with him, *na'am*."

Shaykh Muhammad Ibn Haadee al-Madkhalee, may Allaah preserve him, was also asked this question and he answered by saying: "I think that anyone who wears these hairstyles will be thought bad of, it should be avoided, and we all know that the Messenger of Allaah, *sallAllahu 'alayhi wa sallam,* loved to oppose the Jews, Christians, and the rest of polytheists whenever he could, in all of his matters and affairs...”

Q. 14: The prison administration here has agreed to provide the incarcerated Muslims who wish to follow up the fasting *Ramadaan* with six days of voluntary fasting in the month of *Shawaal* with food to break their fast and also with dinner meals, however with the condition that these days be fasted consecutively stating that it may be difficult upon them to distribute the food and meals throughout the various days of the rest of the month. Also, many of the brothers here don't have the ability to buy snacks and meals in the month of *Shawaal,* so the question is: Is it lawful to participate in fasting along with this stipulation that they have placed on us?

A. 14: Shaykh 'Abdul-'Azeez 'Aqeel answered: “This is fine, *al-Hamdulillaah*; this is a good thing and there isn't anything wrong with participating with this agreement and condition because of the circumstance which the prison administration states, being that it would be rather difficult to give the *iftaar* and means during the various days throughout the month.”

Q. 15: Here in our prison, we have a very large room or hall that is currently empty which we have taken as a *musalla*, rather we have called a masjid, and no one other than the Muslims are allowed to use this hall for any purpose that doesn't pertain to Islaam. Also, the prison administration allows us to use this hall or room for establishing *jumu'ah,* congregational prayers, and the *'eid* prayer, however we don't own this room or hall, So accordingly, is the Muslim who enters this hall required to offer two units of prayer before he sits down or not?

A. 15: Shaykh 'Abdul-'Azeez 'Aqeel answered: "No, you don't have to make the two *raka'ahs* before sitting down."

Q. 16: "I have a store in the prison and I sell all types of products such as, foods and snacks, cleaning, hygienic products, etc... I buy the merchandise wholesale and then sell it making a fifty-percent profit; so is this lawful?"

A. 16: Shaykh Wasiyullaah al-'Abbaas answered: "Why does there have to be a fifty-percent increase? Is this a must that he gets this percentage as profit? Is the price of these products after buying and increasing fifty percent considered extremely high or not ordinary, rather this is regular then this is okay, as for if he only puts this fifty percent increase and the price becomes extremely costly and he is taking advantage of the weakness of the inmates and their lack of money, then this is not lawful and he must avoid it, *na'am.*"

Q. 17: "We all know that the *Mushaf* should not be taken into filthy places, however, the toilet is inside of the prison cell and we can't remove it or take it further away, but he have closets and drawers, so my question is: Is it binding or best to put the *Mushaf* inside of the closet or drawer when we answer the call of nature?"

A. 17: Shaykh Wasiyullaah al-'Abbaas answered: "*Insha Allah,* this is best, but not mandatory. In this situation, you are only required to fear Allaah to the best of your ability."

Q. 18: "With regards to the toilet being inside of the cell, we have heard that it is binding that we cover the toilet seat while offering the prayer because the Jinn congregate around the toilet. Is there any origin to this speech in our religion?"

A. 18: Shaykh Wasiyullaah al-'Abbaas answered: "No, this is incorrect. It is not binding that you cover the toilet seat while offering the prayer. What is important is that you don't offer the prayer over the toilet seat, or any other filthy, impure place, *na'am*."

Q. 19: "Here at our prison we go out to the yard for exercise and play, and there aren't any water faucets or running water except only three large water coolers for drinking. In the seven years that I have been at this prison I have seen many inmates pass out because of dehydration and extreme thirst. So my question is, In this circumstance is it lawful for us to perform *tayammum* for the prayer instead of *wudoo,* or not? I have read that some scholars have allowed this if the water that a person has is only for drinking?"

A. 19: Shaykh 'Abdullaah al-Jarboo' answered: "There is detail for this answer: Firstly: If you don't have to exercise and/or play, or just exercise just a little, I mean the least amount with which you can keep up on your health, and therefore not need to drink a lot of water which will allow you to perform *wudoo* with the water, then it is not permissible for you to perform *tayammum*. Instead you have to offer *wudoo* with this water, even if it is for drinking, whereas there isn't a dire necessity in which you have to keep all of the water, and if you don't you will perish because of extreme thirst or dehydration. Secondly: If you know for sure, or are almost sure, that you will have enough time to leave the yard and return back to your cells or the area in which you offer the prayer before the prescribed time of the prayer leaves and offer *wudoo* with water, then you are allowed to do this. Thirdly: As for if you must exercise and you are in need of this water to drink and if you don't you may pass out or possibly perish, then you are allowed to perform *tayammum* instead of offering *wudoo* just as the people of knowledge have mentioned with regards to this matter and Allaah knows best."

Q. 20: "Is it lawful for us Muslim men to marry women from the people of the scripture, the Jews and Christians?"

A. 20: Shaykh 'Ubayd al-Jaabiree, may Allaah preserve him, answered: "I cannot say that this is unlawful, however there lies no doubt that it is much better and purer for you to marry the female Believers. Do not be deceived or taken by the beauty of some of those Jewish or Christian women; the Believing women are better for you if you only knew."

Q. 21: Should those following the *Imaam* in the prayer say the *tasleem* out loud or to themselves?

A. 21: Al-'Allaamah 'Abdul-Mushin al-'Abbaad al-Badr, may Allaah extol his life upon good and obedience, answered: "No, those who are following the *Imaam* in the Prayer should say the *tasleem* silently to themselves, just like the rest of what they say behind the *Imaam* such as: "*Rabbanaa lakal-Hamd*", and the rest of the *takbeeraat* of moving from pillar to pillar...*na'am*."

[103]

Q. 22: Is it permissible for Muslim women to marry Muslim brothers who are incarcerated? And if so, then is it something that is recommended?

A. 22: Shaykh Saalih' as-Sindee, may Allaah preserve him, said: "As for the validity of the contract, then there isn't anything in the Sharee'ah making it unlawful or invalid; if he entrusts someone for the contract, or does it himself through the different means [such as a letter or phone call], this is something that is lawful and correct in the *Sharee'ah*. As for what do I think about it and is it a good thing? Then possibly it will be a good thing as long as the woman is pleased with this agreement and he is honest with her and tells her the truth about his duration in the prison. He must be up front and honest with her about how many years he will be incarcerated. If he has five, seven, or ten years, then he must tell her this from day one, before the contract. So if she knows about this, is aware of this reality, and is pleased this, then no problem; for surely, marriage may assist the incarcerated brother upon his religion in the prison. This could produce for him a means of hope and aspiration to improve himself more in the institution and have something to look forward to when he comes home. Also writing his wife and speaking with her may soothe his soul and mind along with pleasing feelings and sooth her soul and mind outside the prison. Sometimes marriage goes deeper than physical unity, but it has a big effect on the heart and soul, *na'am*."

Q. 23: Here, during *Ramadaan* the Prison feed us after *iftaar* and provides us with bagged food for *suhoor*. We also get to pray *Maghrib* in congregation...the one condition is that we sign a 'contract' agreeing to comply with the various legislated obligations

during fasting. So the first question is: Is it permissible for us to sign this contract? The second question is: If one of us breaks a rule laid down in the Book & the *Sunnah,* then are we still allowed to participate in accepting the food and praying in congregation or not, or should we just buy our own food from commissary and fast individually?

A. 23: Shaykh Muhammad Ibn Haadee, may Allaah preserve him, said: "There is no problem in signing this contract; this is okay. As for if one of you committed a sin or fell into something that opposes the rules of the *Sharee'ah* regarding fasting or the likes, then he is allowed to eat the food and participate with his brothers, and perhaps Allaah will forgive him and pardon him via making *taubah,* and *al-Hamdulillaah,* Allaah has screened him and covered his shortcomings and sins, *na'am.*"

Q. 24: What do we say to those who claim that calling yourself *Salafee* is an innovation?

A. 24: Shaykh Muhammad Ibn Haadee al-Madkhalee, may Allaah preserve him, said: "This is wrong and incorrect, rather what did *Shaykhul-Islaam* Ibn Taymiyyah says: "There isn't any blame upon the individual who manifests the method of the *Salaf,* ascribes and affiliates himself thereto..." The questioner asked: "So o our Shaykh, we should make this famous saying of Ibn Taymiyyah the response to this doubt?"[263] The Shaykh responded: "*Na'am...*So therefore,

---

[263] The entire saying of Shaykhul-Islaam, may Allaah be pleased with him, can be found in *"al-Majmoo'"* (vol. 4/pg. 149) it reads: "There isn't any blame upon the individual who manifests the method of the *Salaf,* ascribes and affiliates himself thereto. Rather, it is incumbent for this to be=

calling yourself *Salafee* is for the purpose of *tamyeez* [distinguishing
yourself] from the deviant sects and parties of the Muslims and
those who claim to be Muslims. We call ourselves *Salafee* this for
this purpose, and there is no problem in saying this. The questioner
says: "O Shaykh, even many of the disbelievers know the difference
between the *Salafees* and the non-*Salafees*...for example when we go
back to America and we are asked in the airport by the customs or
FBI: "What type of Muslim are you?" We respond: "We are
Salafees." So that they can know that we aren't with the groups of
terrorism and suicide bombers, etc...So they say: "Oh, okay we know
the *Salafees*, good..." The Shaykh replied: "Allaahu Akbar! You see,
this is from the fruits of clarifying the truth and spreading what is
correct, even these disbelievers understand this *tamyeez*..." It is also
extremely important that your actions be like the actions of the
Salaf, your character and etiquettes and everything that you say and
do in the Religion. Unfortunately, there are many people who say
this word and attribute themselves to the way of the *Salaf* and they
are from the furthest people from being like the *Salaf* in that which
they say and do. You must be *Salafee* in your practice of Islaam...set
the example with your deeds and actions..."

❁ ❁ ❁

=accepted from him by unanimous agreement [of the People of
Knowledge] because the method of the *Salaf* is nothing but the truth."

Questions Related to Gangs[264]

Q. 36: In the United States of America, there are non-Islamic
radical groups erupting from one end of the country to the other.
One group in particular is involved in drug selling, unlawful
killings, robberies, oppression, kidnapping, and an array of other
crimes on all levels.

Their creed is based on an acronym which spells out [B.L.O.O.D. -
Brotherly Love Overrides Oppression and Destruction]. Their
Manhaaj (methodology) is specific to what is mentioned above,
and they have to adhere to the commands of their leaders. Also,
their initiation could be from harming or killing a Muslim or the
general people. This is a growing problem here in the U.S.A. of
great magnitude.

Unfortunately many of the Muslim youth of this country have
faithfully accepted the creed of this non-Islamic radical group or
their likes and live their lives abiding by the creed of these groups
and refuse to abandon that creed. The Muslims have been
advising the Muslim youth to denounce this behavior, but it has
been to no avail. They believe it is permissible to follow the creed
of Islaam and follow the creed of this non-Islamic radical group
and when you advise them against this behavior they say, "I
believe in Allaah, and I am still a Muslim."

---

[264] These questions were taken from the book "Islamic Ruling for the
incarcerated muslims"

My question is because of their allegiance to the *Kufar* (non-Muslims) and their creed... do we allow them to offer *Salaat* (prayer) in congregation with us and attend *Jumu'ah*? Do we give them *Salaams* or respond to *Salaams* from them? Should we boycott them? Should we offer *Janaazah* (funeral prayer) for them (when they die)? Are they considered apostates?

So do we allow them to offer *Salaat* (prayer) in congregation with us and attend *Jumu'ah* (the obligatory Friday congregational prayer)?

A. 36: Shaykh 'Umar as-Sumaalee, may Allaah preserve him, responded: "Yes."

Q. 37: Do we give them *Salaams* or respond to *Salaams* from them?

A. 37: "Yes."

Q. 38: Should we boycott them?

A. 38: "As for the younger ones of them, we should be cordial to them and give them *Naseehah* (advice) as much as possible. The older ones of them we should not become friendly with. Give them *Naseehah* and keep our distance; beware of them because they are of the age to know the effects of their criminal actions."

Q. 39: Should we offer *Janaazah* (the funeral paryer) for them (when they die)?

A. 39: "Yes. If another group of the Muslims, other than the *Salafees* are willing to perform their *Janaazah*, this is best. But if not, it is incumbent upon us. *Fard Kifayah* (an obligatory responsibility in which, if a group of Muslims performs it, it lifts the responsibility from the rest of the Muslims' obligation to perform it)."

Q. 40: Are they considered apostates?

A. 40: "No. These people are to be considered members of a gang. If they were known to be Muslims and then went on to join this gang, we still must consider them to be Muslims. We do not know what is in their hearts. From the acts that they are attributed with, the members of this gang are criminals, and as such, if it were allowed, then they should be punished. But we know that we are not allowed to punish them in the land of the non-Muslims. We must give them *Naseehah* (advice), with *Sabr* (patience)."

Questions Related to the Nation of Islaam[265]

Q. 43: Members of the Nation of Islaam are starting to visit the Masajid of the *Salafees.* Although this group considers themselves to be Muslims, they believe that Allaah came in the person of Fard Muhammad (i.e. incarnate). It is good that they are coming and listening to the truth, but my question is should we allow them to pray with us with this incorrect *'Aqeedah* (creed) for the sake of *Da'wah* (calling them to Islaam) so as not to hurt their feelings and run them away as some brothers feel? Or should we remove them from the rows and explain to them why (we removed them) with proofs from the Qur'aan and *Sunnah?* Please clarify for us the correct thing to do?

A. 43a: Shaykh 'Abdullaah al-Bukhaaree, may Allaah preserve him, answered:

"If these people are coming to learn about the correct *'Aqeedah* (creed or beliefs) then they should not be removed. They believe that they are Muslims even though they are not.

So they should be treated as the *Munaafiqoon* were treated at the time of the Prophet, *sallAllahu 'alayhi wa sallam.* The hypocrites prayed in the ranks of the Muslims and they were well known to the Messenger, *sallAllahu 'alayhi wa sallam,* as well as Hudhayfah,

---

[265] This question is from the book "Islamic Ruling for the incarcerated muslims"

[110]

radiyallaahu 'anhu. They should be taught and allowed to pray with the Muslims."

A. 43b: This question was also posed to Shaykh Muhammad bin Haadee, may Allaah preserve him, and he answered:

"They should be allowed to pray initially if they are coming to learn about the correct *'Aqeedah*. And the first thing that they should be taught about is the falseness of the *'Aqeedah* of Elijah Muhammad and the truth about Islaam. So if they accept what is taught to them, they will enter into the fold of Islaam and if not, then they should not be allowed to pray with the Muslims."

Shaykh Muhammad bin Haadee, may Allaah preserve him, was then asked, "How long should the Muslims be patient with them?"

The Shaykh replied:

"As long as it takes to teach them that which is correct, and the proof is established."

The Shaykh was then asked, "If removing them is going to cause bigger problems, perhaps leading to the intervention of the authorities, the Muslims not being able to use the masjid, or other than that, what should be done?"

The Shaykh replied:

"It is a must to weigh the benefit and the harm in the likes of these situations and for the Muslim to have foresight. So if removing

them is going to bring a greater evil, patience must be enacted. And
Allaah knows best."

Questions Related to Marriage, Intercourse and Masturbation[266]

Q. 44: In terms of a Muslim man marrying a Christian woman, would the *Imaam* of the community to which the Muslim man belongs, act as the *Walee* for the Christian woman (i.e., when she has no *Walee*)? Or what is the procedure? Can a Muslim male be a *Walee* for a non-Muslim woman, or can she have a non-Muslim male as her *Walee*?

Also, is there any difference in procedure between a Muslim man that marries a Muslim woman, and where a Muslim man marries a Christian woman?

A. 44: Shaykh Muhammad bin Haadee, may Allaah preserve him, answered:

"If the Christian woman has no *Walee*, then the leader of the Islaamic Center or *Imaam* of the *Masjid* would act as her *Walee*. There is no harm in the Muslim being the *Walee* of the People of the Book (Jews and Christians) however, the opposite is forbidden.

This is due to the fact that the Muslim is better than the *Kaafir* and Allaah says what means, '*And never will Allaah grant to the disbelievers a way (to triumph) over the believers.*' *[Sooratun-Nisaa (4):141]*. And Allaah knows best."

---

[266] These questions have been quoted from "Islaamic Rulings for Incarcerated Muslims vol. 1" with slight adjustment

Q. 45: It is acknowledged and confirmed that masturbation is not permissible in Islaam. However, this is a chronic endeavor in prison amongst those who do not possess the means of obtaining a wife and whom are sentenced to twenty, thirty, and forty years. What is the ruling for those who fall into this category?

A. 45: Shaykh Ahmad Bazmool, may Allaah preserve him, responded:

In the *Hadeeth* of the Prophet, *sallAllahu 'alayhi wa sallam*, he said:

'O young men, whoever is able from you to get married, then let him get married and that is for protecting his private parts and (lowering) his gaze. And whoever is not able to get married then let him take to fasting.'

Based on this advice from the Prophet, *sallAllahu 'alayhi wa sallam*, the first and foremost thing that the brothers in prison should do is take to fasting. If the fasting does not take away the urge to masturbate then he should eat only a little bit to break his fast and do not eat a lot at night. That is because eating a lot of food is something that increases the desires. So he should keep the eating to a minimum. If that is not helping and he needs to do more to protect himself, then he should stay away from the affairs that are found there in the prison. For example, television, or other things that will possibly lead him to being in a situation where his desires are being a diversion for him. He should stay away from any external affairs that may distract him and cause him to think about those desires that would lead him to masturbate. Let him increase his *Salaah* (prayer), recitation of the Qur'aan, and reading in

general, so that *Shaytaan* does not have the chance to play with him.
If all of these things have not helped and there is still the desire to
masturbate, then his situation will be of four cases:

1. He is a person who has done all of these things but he will
   still fall into masturbation just out of desire. He is able to
   prevent it, but he likes it so he does it. This case is clearly
   Haraam.

2. He masturbates because is he afraid that he may fall into
   something *Haraam* like homosexuality. It is not something
   that is going to happen, it is not something he is sure is
   going to happen, so he has to divert himself from it. If this
   is the case, that he is afraid he may fall into it, then this
   case of masturbation is still *Haraam*.

3. The third case is that of certainty. He knows for sure that if
   he does not masturbate, then he will fall into some
   homosexuality or some great sin. If he is certain that he
   will fall into something bigger than masturbation, in this
   case, it would be permissible to masturbate just enough to
   keep him away from that sin just in the time of *Haajah*
   (need).

4. There is another case where masturbation would be
   permissible. This is the case when, if he is a person who
   has reached a point where he is basically boiling inside, or
   he is about to explode. Maybe he will not go into sin but
   he himself cannot take it anymore. It is something that he
   cannot stand anymore. If it's really like that, then he

[115]

masturbates enough to rid this from him, so that he can be free of this type of situation. Then this is permissible under necessity. It is important to note that from the problems that arise from masturbation, is that he becomes a person who is physically weak. He is a person who has weak sperm. He is a person who begins to have uncertainty about his body potency. He becomes barren. His penis and eyesight will become weak as well. There are a number of medical things that are the direct result of a person masturbating. So I wanted to mention these because sometimes a person does not think about the punishment of the Hereafter but if you mention to him something about what will happen to him in the *Dunya* (worldly life), he will appreciate it more."

Examples of Patience and Perseverance While Incarcerated from the Trials of Imaam Ahmad

In the beginning of the third century after the *Hijrah*, a group from the *Mu'talizah* sect got very close to the *khaleefah* of the Muslims, al Ma'moon Ibn Haaroon ar-Rasheed, until the point that they caused him to deviate from the creed of the *Salaf* upon which were the *khaleefahs* before him, of both the *Umayyad* [al-Umawee] and *Abbasid* [al-'Abbasee] dynasties. They drove him into false beliefs and made fair to him the statement that, "the Qur'aan was created" and negating Allaah's attributes along with other deviant beliefs.

Approximately in the year 218H, al-Ma'moon wrote to his assistant, the governor of Baghdad, Ishaaq Ibn Ibraaheem Ibn Mus'ab, ordering him to call the people to profess the statement that "the Qur'aan is created."

He [the governor of Baghdad] therefore gathered the jurists and Imaams of Hadeeth of Baghdad and read upon them al-Ma'moon's request. The scholars refused this order greatly, so Ibraaheem Ibn Ishaaq began to threaten them with imprisonment, torture, harsh beatings, sanctions and the likes.

Some scholars gave in to the threats and torture, and said that "the Qur'aan was created" based on the allowance to commit an act of disbelief when being coerced. Others refused and chose imprisonment and torture, at the head of them was Imaam Ahmad Ibn Hanbal, may Allaah be pleased with him and his brothers from the Imaams of Hadeeth of his time. There wasn't any *imaam* who remained more firm, patient and rigid through this horrid period of

Islamic history than Imaam Aboo 'Abdillaah, *rahimahullaah*. So they
were imprisoned, and many of them did not make it out due to the
harsh beatings and conditions in the prisons. Imaam Ahmad was
beaten several times and died with the deep scars of the severe
lashings. But al-Ma'moon died before Imaam Ahmad reached him,
so he was sent back to Baghdad. Afterwards, the succeeding
khaleefahs undertook the trial and torture, al-Mu'tasim, al-Waathiq,
up until the reign of al- Mutawakkil; the *khaleefah* relieved the
imaams of the *Sunnah* of the punishment and put an end to gloomy
turmoil.

For this reason did Ibn al-Jauzee, *rahimahullaah*, say: "Al-Mutawakkil
extinguished the fire of the *bid'ah* and lit the lamps of the *Sunnah*."

With relief brought by Allaah via the hands of al-Mutawakkil,
Imaam Ahmad, *rahimahullaah*, was enabled to revive his call to the
creed of the *Salaf*.

Let's now look at some of what is mentioned and narrated from
Imaam Ahmad during his imprisonment and lashing and reflect on
his patience, firmness, steadfastness and resolve, along with his hope
and longing that he had for the reward and relief from Allaah,
Mighty and Magnificent.

Muhammad Ibn Ibraaheem al-Booshanjee, *rahimahullaah*, said: "In
ar-Raqqah [a city in north central Syria], they began to remind Aboo
'Abdillaah about the allowance of verbally affirming to save oneself,
and the reports regarding that. So he replied: 'What will you do
with the *hadeeth* narrated by Khabbaab that reads, '**Amongst those
who came before you a man would be sawn in half, but that would**

not cause him to abandon his religion.' So we gave up hope
regarding him.' He also said: 'I don't care about imprisonment,
since it and my home are the same, nor about being beheaded, but
rather I fear the trial of the whip." So a fellow prisoner heard him
and said, 'don't be concerned, O Aboo 'Abdullaah, *rahimahullaah*,
for it will only take two lashes, then after that you won't notice the
rest of them strike you.' So it was as if he felt at peace because of
this." Saalih, *rahimahullaah*, the son of Imaam Ahmad,
rahimahullaah, said, "My father and Muhammad Ibn Nooh,
rahimahummullaah, were taken from Baghdad in chains."

He also reported that his father was asked: "O Abaa 'Abdillaah,
rahimahullaah, if you are threatened with the sword will you
consent?'" He replied, 'No.'

He also reported: "...And my father was taken to Baghdad in chains
and remained a few days in Yaasiriyyah. Then he was imprisoned in
a house hired by the house of 'Umaarah. Then he was moved to
the general prison in Mausiliyyah Street, and he said, 'I used to lead
the prisoners in the prayer and I was chained.'"

This shows us how he remained to practice his religion and strictly
guard the congregational prayer in those difficult, harsh conditions.
The situations of the jails and prisons today without the least doubt
are nothing compared to the conditions of those of the past.
Therefore, my noble brothers, hold fast to the Sunnah during all
circumstances and situations to the best of your ability and know for
sure that Allaah is with His Believing slaves.

It is reported that Imaam Ahmad, *rahimahullaah,* remained in prison for about thirty months and that many of his comrades used to come to him and read books to him in the prison.

Hanbal, *rahimahullaah,* reported: "...and he was severely restricted in his imprisonment and fell ill in *Ramadaan.* Then after a short while he was moved to the general prison. He remained in prison for about thirty months. We used to come to him and read the book of *al-Irjaa'* to him and other books while in the prison. I saw him lead them in the prayer in chains. He would take his foot out of the main manacle during the times of prayer and sleep." The lesson that we can derive from this is seeking and reviewing knowledge in prison.

Narrated Saalih Ibn Ahmad, *rahimahullaah:* "My father said: 'Each day two men would come to me. They would not cease debating with me, and when they finished they would call for another shackle to be added to a shoe already upon me, so that there were four upon my legs... Then on the fourth night al-Mu'tasim commanded Ishaaq, *rahimahullaah,* to convey me to him, so I was entered upon by Ishaaq, He said, 'O Ahmad, by Allaah, it is your life that you are to lose. He will not kill you with the sword. He desires, if you do not consent and agree with him, to lash you continually, and then kill you in a place where neither the sun nor the moon can be seen.'"

Imaam Ahmad, *rahimahullaah,* went on in narrating the story: 'We came to the place known as 'The Gate of the Garden.' I was taken out and placed upon a riding beast in my chain. There was nobody there to hold me, so more than once I nearly feel off upon my face due to the weight of the chains.'"

Imaam Ahmad, *rahimahullaah*, said that once his arms were stretched to commence the lashing: "So the flogging posts were brought forward and my arms were stretched, and someone behind me said, 'Seize the two pommels of the frame and hold them tightly,' but I didn't understand what he said, so my arms became dislocated."

Despite this stressful and fearful situation awaiting him, he remained patient and content, realizing that no one could harm or save him save Allaah, the Exalted.

Narrated Muhammad Ibn Ibraaheem al-Booshanjee, *rahimahullaah*: "They mentioned that when al-Mu'tasim saw them tie Ahmad, *rahimahullaah*, to the flogging posts, and he saw how he remained firm and resolute he [al-Mu'tasim] began feeling relentless.

Al-Mu'tasim, *rahimahullaah*, would say to the lashers: "Strike him with severity."

Imaam Ahmad, *rahimahullaah*, was continuously lashed until he became unconscious. Once he regained consciousness a man who was present said to him, "We threw you down upon your face, and threw a mat upon your back and trampled upon you." Imaam Ahmad was not aware of that. Keeping in mind that he, *rahimahullaah*, was fasting and refused to break his fast even after this strenuous lashing. They have narrated that he led the prayer when his wounds were pouring forth with blood.

[121]

Whether Imaam Ahmad, *rahimahullaah,* fasted or was prevented from receiving food and drink, he continued to remain patient and sharp. His son Saalih *rahimahullaah,* narrated: "A man who was present with him informed me that he had no food during those three days [when they debated with him and lashed him], but he didn't make a slip with regards to a single word. He said, 'And I didn't think that anyone could have the courage and strength of heart that he did.'"

Imaam Ahmad, *rahimahullaah,* also said: "I became unconscious a number of times."

It is said that the total number of lashes that he received was approximately thirty four. Once he was released and allowed home, he was taken to the cellar. One who specialized in wounds and their treatment was brought in, and said, 'I have seen men who have received a thousand lashes, but I have never seen a case as bad as this...' and he would come to treat him. His face had been struck more than once, and he remained flat upon his face for as long as Allaah willed. Then the man said to him, 'There is some flesh here which I must cut.' So he brought an iron tool and would hold the flesh with it and cut it with a knife, and Ahmad, *rahimahullaah,* bore all of this, only raising his voice with the praise of Allaah, and he was cured. However he continued to feel pain in some places, and the marks of the lashing were clearly visible on his back until he died."

The point from all of this is that this great Imaam remained patient upon the countless hardships, severe trials and great turmoil, stood firm and lost not hope of Allaah's mercy. All of this was done for the service and defense of Islaam, and preserving the sound creed for the generations of Muslims to come. Reading the stories of the people of the past is not only a means of realizing their virtue upon this nation, but also a means of soothing and comfort for the mind and the soul. Looking at what they went through and what was the great purpose of that enormous sacrifice.

There are countless virtues of patience that are mentioned in the Book and the *Sunnah*, and ample statements of the *Salaf* as explained by the people of knowledge. Therefore, o my noble, brother, be patient while in prison and let the statement of the Prophet, *sallAllahu 'alayhi wa sallam*, constantly stay on your mind, which reads:

"Indeed, the affair of the Believer is quite amazing! All of it is good for him and this isn't for anyone besides the Believer; if prosperity comes his way he is thankful and is therefore good for him, and if adversity befalls him he is patient and it is therefore good for him."[267]

---

[267] Collected by Muslim-summarized-(no. 2092), on the authority of Suhayb ar-Roomee, *radiyAllaahu 'anhu*.

Lessons and Morals from the Imprisonment of Shaykhul-Islaam Ibn Taymiyyah, *rahimahullaah*

In the name of Allaah, the Most Merciful, the Granter of Mercy. All praise belongs and are due to Allaah, the Lord of the Worlds. May prayers and salutations be extolled upon our Prophet Muhammad and all of his followers and companions, to proceed...

It is reported that Imaam ash-Shaafi'ee, may Allaah have mercy on him, said: "Time is like a sword, if you use it properly [i.e. take advantage of it and invest it in good] it will cut you."

Time is the greatest blessing and grandest bounty of Allaah upon His slaves. It is the most valuable gift that He has ever bestowed upon His servants, whereas with time they were able to worship, laud and praise Him. With time, they have been enabled to actualize the purpose behind their creation which is to worship Him, alone without any partner.

Therefore, it is upon the Muslim in general and the incarcerated Muslim in special to utilize his time in that which will come back to him in profit and benefit.

O my noble brother, use your time during your stay in prison wisely and remember that there will come a time in which you don't have the free time that you currently have. Rather, there will come a time in which you will stand in front of Allaah, and you will be asked about your time and how you spent it.

Narrated by Aboo Barzah al-Aslamee, *radiyAllaahu 'anhu*, the Prophet, *sallAllahu 'alayhi wa sallam*, said: **"The feet of the son of Aadam will not go away until he is asked about four things."** [He mentioned from the four]: **"And about his life how did he spend it and about his youth what did he do with it."**[268]

Free time is from the countless bounties of Allaah that most people are in loss regarding. Narrated Ibn 'Abbaas, *radiyAllaahu 'anhumma*, the Prophet, *sallAllahu 'alayhi wa sallam*, said: **"Two bounties many people are in loss regarding: good health and free time."**[269]

Allaah, the Exalted, has already blessed many, if not most of you, mighty brothers by guiding you to the true religion of al-Islaam and saving you from entering the Fire eternally abiding therein. Then out of His generosity, He has blessed you again by guiding you to the *Sunnah* of His Messenger, *sallAllahu 'alayhi wa sallam*, and way of the *Salaf*.

From thanking Allaah is that you use your time in that which pleases Him. Let us look at how a man used his time in prison and looked at it as one of the biggest of Allaah's favors upon him: Said al-Haafidh, Ibn Qayyimil-Jauziyyah, *rahimahullaah*, "I heard Shaykhul-Islaam Ibn Taymiyyah, may Allaah have mercy on him, saying: 'Verily, there is a garden in the life of this world. Whoever doesn't enter it will not enter the garden in the hereafter.'

---

[268] Collected by at-Tirmidhee (no. 2417). Imaam at-Tirmidhee declared this hadeeth to be authentic, similarly Shaykh al-Albaanee.
[269] Collected by al-Bukhaaree (no. 6049).

I also heard him saying once, 'what can my enemies do to me?! My paradise and garden is in my breast, wherever I go it is with me; it never leaves me. If they lock me up, then it is a perfect opportunity to seclude myself for the worship of Allaah, if they kill me then I will be martyred, and if they exile me from my homeland then it will be a vacation'."

He also used to say in his sitting that he held in the citadel in which he was imprisoned: "If I spent in gold the likes of which amounts the size of this citadel, I would not see that I have repaid them for this favor, or what they have been a reason behind of good." Or the likes of this meaning.

He used to say very often while making *sujood* in the prison, "O Allaah! Aid me upon thanking You and perfecting my worship for You."

Once he said to me: "The inmate in reality is he whose heart has been incarcerated from his Lord, and the captive in reality is he who has been taken captive by his own lusts."

When he entered the citadel and he was behind the gates, he looked unto it and recited: *"So a wall will be put up between them, with a gate therein. Inside it will be mercy, and outside it will be torment."* [*Soorah al-Hadeed (57): 13*]

Surely, Allaah knows that I have never seen anyone living a happier life than him [his teacher, Shaykhul-Islaam Ibn Taymiyyah, *rahimahullaah*] despite what he used to go through of difficulties, lack of luxury and pleasure. Instead, he went through the exact

[126]

opposite of that such as being imprisoned, threatened and exhausted. Despite all of this, he was from amongst those who led the best lives, with one of the most expanded breasts, strongest hearts and happiest souls; the bloom of happiness was visible upon his face. Moreover, whenever we became afraid of something, or had negative thoughts of what would happen to us in the future or we felt confined in the land we would go to him and it wasn't long after we saw him or heard his speech that all of those worries would go away and would turn into means of the expansion or our breasts, strength, certainty and tranquility.

So how Perfect and Free from all defects is He Who has shown His slaves His garden before they actually meet Him, and opened up for them its gates in the abode for working deeds [i.e. the worldly life], so He sent on them from its fragrance and gentle breeze and its perfume that which made them exert all of their energy for the sole purpose of seeking and racing unto it." [270]

Once, he wrote to some of his friends while in prison a letter in which he said: "All of that which Allaah, the Exalted, decrees and ordains entails total good, mercy and wisdom. My Lord is Ever Courteous to whom He wills and He is the Ever Powerful, the All Mighty, the All-Knowing, and the All Wise. Moreover, harm never falls upon an individual except because of his own sins. [Allaah, the Exalted, says:] *"Whatever befalls you of good is only from Allaah and whatever befalls you of evil is only from yourself"* [Soorah an-Nisaa (4): 79] Therefore, it is binding upon the slave to constantly thank Allaah and praise Him no matter what his situation may be,

---

[270] *"al-Waabil as-Sayyib"* (vol. 1/pg. 67)

and seek forgiveness for his sins. Showing thankfulness demands an increase in Allaah's favors and bounties, and seeking forgiveness wards off punishments and vices.

[The slave must realize and constantly remind himself that] Allaah does not ordain anything for the Believer except that it is good for him, if some prosperity comes his way he shows thanks, and if some adversity befalls him then he is patient; thus all of that happens to him is good for him."[271]

Therefore, you, o my blessed brother, should not look at your incarceration as a misfortune. Instead you should look at it as blessings from Allaah and free time that can be used to rectify what has transpired in your life by offering sincere repentance and asking Allaah to give you time from your life which is better and more blessed in the future than that of the past.

---

[271] "Majmoo al-Fataawaa" (vol. 28/pg. 47-48)

Lessons and Morals from the Imprisonment of Shaykh Muhammad Naasirud-Deen al-Albaanee, *rahimahullaah*

We previously expounded on some examples of utilizing your time while incarcerated with what Ibn Qayyim, *rahimahullaah*, narrated to us from the state of Shaykhul-Islaam Ibn Taymiyyah, may Allaah have mercy on them. Now let's take an example from one of our contemporary scholars, the noble *imaam* and great scholar of *Hadeeth*, the reviver of the *Sunnah* of our time, Shaykh Muhammad Naasirud-Deen al-Albaanee, *rahimahullaah*. When we look into his biography, we find that he was imprisoned numerous times and went though great hardships and difficulties in the path of reviving, spreading and defending the *Sunnah*, may Allaah be pleased with Him and reward him well on our behalf, *aameen*. Listen to him as he narrates to us some of that:

"... Whereas He [Allaah, the Exalted] had ordained upon me to be imprisoned in the year 1389 A.H./1969 C.E. along with numerous other scholars without any crime that we committed besides calling to Islaam and teaching it to the people. I was jailed in the Citadel and other prisons in Damascus. I was let out for some time only to be locked up again and driven out to the Peninsula to stay in its prison for several months, all of which I hope for the reward from Allaah, the Mighty and Magnificent.

Allaah had certainly decreed that I only had with me one of my favorite books "*Saheeh Muslim*", a pencil and eraser. There I devoted all of my time to fulfilling my dream which was summarizing it. I finished this task in just three months, working night and day without any fatigue or weariness. As a result, what the enemies of this nation had intended to be a punishment for me backfired against them and turned out to be a blessing for us of which the students of knowledge in which the Muslims can rest in its pleasant shade in all places. So all praise is due to Allaah, He Whom all righteous deeds are achieved and perfected.

Likewise, Allaah, the Exalted, had facilitated for me free time to fulfill numerous knowledge based tasks that I was unable to give them their due time during my normal life out of prison, whereas some of the governments prevented me from going on my normal trips that I would take to visit different towns and cities in Syria for the purpose of calling to the Book and the *Sunnah*, which is known as "house arrest", just as I was prevented time to time from teaching my many lessons which I had to spend a lot of time in preparation for. All of which relieved me of many tasks, jobs and meeting large numbers of people that used to take a great deal of my time..."[272]

Here we see how the scholars of the later generations adopted the path of those of the earlier generations. Look how Shaykh al-Albaanee, *rahimahullaah*, turned what many people look at as a vice and misfortune into a virtue and bounty?! If he and others patiently persevered while in prison for calling to the Book and the *Sunnah*, then how patient should the one who is imprisoned for committing a crime against his own self and Allaah's creation be? So let us take the lesson from this story which is utilizing your time while incarcerated. He only had a pencil and an eraser! What have you done with the resources that Allaah has endowed you with? In the prison, you have countless sources and references to aid you in the path of seeking knowledge, nourishing and purifying your soul. So

---

[272] "*Mukhtasar Saheeh al-Bukhaaree*" (Vol. 1/pg. ٥)

my advice to myself first and you o my noble brother secondly, is to
busy yourself with the Book of Allaah and authentic *Sunnah* of His
Messenger, *sallAllahu 'alayhi wa sallam*, and all sciences that assist
you in understanding the two. Fill your day with the remembrance
of Allaah, reading His words and increasing in knowledge and
righteous actions. Place a book or two beneath your pillow and try
to make it your habit not to go to sleep except after reading fifteen
or twenty minutes, reflecting upon what you read. May Allaah bless
us all with beneficial knowledge and righteous actions, indeed He is
the Bestower.

Our Other Publications...

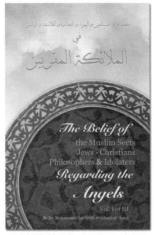

The Belief of the Muslim Sects, Jews....Regarding the Angels
Muhammad ibn 'Abdil-Wahhaab al-'Aqeel - 112pgs. $12.00

A Warning from Wastefulness & Extravagance
Abdul Azeez Ibn Baaz - 46pgs. $6.00

Islam's Solution for the Problems Facing Today's Youth
Muhammad bin Saalih al-'Uthaymeen - 60pgs. $6.00

Explanation Of The Hadeeth "Say,'I Believe In Allah'...
Ibn Rajab Al-Hanbalee - 43pgs. $6.00

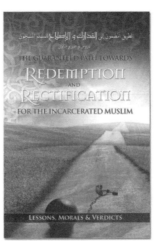

The Guaranteed Path Towards Redemption & Rectification
Various - 132pgs. $12.00

The Best Religion for Mankind....
Shaykh Saalih Al-Fawzaan - 116 pgs $12.00

AUTHENTIC STATEMENTS
PUBLICATIONS

5312 MARKET ST. PHILA, PA 19139

P: 215.382.3382 F: 215.382.3782 E: ORDERS@AUTHENTICSTATEMENTS.COM

www.authenticstatements.com